D0429264

COCKTAIL-SUPPER COOKBOOK

Cocktail-Supper Cookbook

MARION W. FLEXNER

BRAMHALL HOUSE, NEW YORK

For Barbara and John to help them entertain with ease—and pleasure.

This edition is published by Brahmall House, Inc.,
a division of Clarkson N. Potter, Inc.,
by arrangement with M. Barrows and Company, Inc.

(A)

Printed in the United States of America.

Library of Congress Catalog Card Number: 55-9256

CONTENTS

WITH THANKS

To these publications for allowing me to use excerpts and recipes from various articles of mine published by them: *Gourmet, House and Garden, Vogue, Woman's Day,* Fawcett Publications, Inc., Franklin Watts, Inc.

To these hotels and restaurants for special recipes: P. G. Leoni, Quo Vadis Restaurant, London; Sabatini's, Florence; Trocadero, The Hague; Maui Palms Hotel, Maui, T. H.; Kauai Inn, Kauai, T. H.

To these individuals: Mary Snow Abbott, Dorothy Clark, Morris Flexner, Camille Glenn, Helen Leopold, and Isabel McMeekin, my gratitude for reviewing the manuscript and to Mary Ochsner for skillful secretarial assistance.

AND SO, COCKTAIL-SUPPERS

You don't need a kitchen to cook in. You don't need a dining room to eat in. With modern know-how, whether your kitchen is the last word in efficiency or a makeshift affair —say a few electric appliances—you can prepare and serve delectable and outstanding meals.

The era of the formal seated dinner party with numerous courses of rich dishes, served perhaps by butlers and party maids, is drawing to a close. Today you can serve *what* you want, *when* you want, *where* you want. Who cares whether you set out the food in the living room, on the open porch, in front of the fire, on the backyard terrace, in a studio bedroom, or some odd corner with pillows scattered over the floor in place of chairs? Even a dining-room table isn't necessary—bridge tables, nests of tables, folding tables, and individual trays, all pinch-hit nicely.

This revolution in entertaining has come about for many reasons: the change in living conditions—the acute shortage of domestic help—the high cost of food—a dislike of waste—calorie consciousness—the desire of many women to carry on with jobs and also to keep house.

And so the cocktail-supper, big and comprehensive or small and intimate, has emerged as the most practical and inexpensive way of entertaining a group. It is elastic—it can be dressed up or down to fit every pocketbook and occasion. It is casual—guests can drop in for a drink and a snack and then go to another engagement, or remain for the evening and eat as heartily as they wish. Even in a tiny apartment, a dozen or more people at a time can be served comfortably, without help, because most of the food and drink can be prepared beforehand.

The ahead-of-time work is always easy. It is that final flurry that undoes the host or hostess. In Buffet Blueprint, both the beginning homemaker and the experienced cook will find detailed directions for planning simple, tempting cocktail-suppers with a *minimum of last-minute effort.* In Chapters 4, 5, and 6, there are fifty menus composed with this problem well in mind.

The 320 recipes presented here give a cross section of dishes which appeal to a wide variety of tastes. Some are adaptations of foreign foods; others, taken from ancient cookbooks, have been brought up to date; a few are originals; many are unique regional specialties from our own country. All recipes are listed in the index. Each dish for which a recipe is given has been starred in the menus, and the number of servings is indicated. Use your arithmetic to adapt them.

Louisville, Kentucky MARION W. FLEXNER
May, 1955

1 BUFFET BLUEPRINT

If your bank account is ample, you can serve whatever foods strike your fancy, ordering pâté de foie gras with truffles from Strasbourg, sole from Dover, grouse from Edinburgh, or a frozen Cupid's Delight from your local caterer. But it you have to cut corners, if you are on a budget—as most of us are these days—then imagination and ingenuity must make up for lack of cash.

PLAN AHEAD

To serve a distinctive cocktail-supper requires planning plus homework and footwork too. Several days before your party, get out pencil and paper. Problem one is to decide on your menu. Among my menus you will find a carefully selected list of non-run-of-the-mill cocktail-suppers. Glance over them. Each meal includes hors d'oeuvre and a drink, with foods which are "congenial." But these are merely suggestions—don't feel you have to follow them to the letter. You can shuffle the various dishes to suit your needs and the tastes of your friends.

If your guests are conservative, by all means give them

the food they like. If they are diet-watchers, stick to meats without sauces, green vegetables, and salads, with fruit for dessert. But where the company is composed of adventurous gourmets or those who appreciate "different" food, then branch out. Here's your chance to serve an elegant continental supper, an enticing New Orleans specialty, or something exotic from the orient via Hawaii.

And don't let yourself get in a rut! If you serve a group a certain meal on one occasion, have something different next time. I keep a list of my guests and the menus I serve. This avoids repeating specialties.

Build your cocktail-supper around a main dish and have that one filling. You do not have to serve a number of courses or a lot of elaborate foods. Limit your menu to a few choice items, but provide plenty of these for second and third helpings.

It isn't practical to have too many hot dishes at a cocktail-supper when you have no help—two is the limit, plus bread. If you are pressed for oven space, select a brown-and-serve bread, or buy something ready to pop into the oven for brief heating.

Having planned the food, list the items you need to buy. Let one shopping trip suffice, and that two or three days before your party. Until you actually shop, your menu should be tentative. Often a particular item you have listed is out of stock, or the price is prohibitive because it is not in season. So have an open mind; be ready to make substitutions.

STITCHES IN TIME

Do all the cooking you can ahead of time to avoid the last-minute frustration of hostess jitters.

I find a six-quart pressure cooker invaluable and would not attempt a party without it. The cooking time of any boiled food, especially soups, is cut down at least a third, often more, if prepared in this utensil.

An impromptu bar set up where it won't block traffic is another timesaver. Use a card table or any other sturdy table you can spare, cover it with foil or plastic to protect the finish. Place all the liquor, glasses, and bar equipment on it. Let the guests mix their own drinks as the spirits move them—pun intended.

Food warmers are a *must* at the self-service buffet since the food usually has to stand a long time. Chafing dishes, candle warmers, electric warming plates, all are excellent. If you can't beg, borrow, or steal such a gadget when you have your party, you'll have to improvise one. Otherwise you'll spend the whole evening at home over the range.

An electric coffeepot or a pretty tea kettle, plus instant coffee, can be put on the buffet table. Then guests can help themselves and you can avoid trips to the kitchen.

FINAL TOUCHES

No matter how fine the ingredients, what the cost, or how pretty the appearance, if the food you serve isn't properly prepared, it will be a total loss. It isn't necessary to decorate food elaborately, though what you serve should look appetizing. A garnish of parsley, celery leaves, or water cress, a sprinkling of paprika, lend eye- as well as taste-appeal.

Finally, serve hot food very, very hot, and cold food very, very cold.

2 HIGH SPIRITS—HINTS FOR BEGINNERS

If you are well informed on wines and spirits, just skip this. I don't pretend to be an authority. Plenty of excellent books cover the subject. I just want to start you off with some introductory bottles for cooking and table use.

ABOUT WINES

There are white wines and red and a delicate pink one (vin rosé). They are named for the districts where the grapes, from which they are made, were originally grown.

Broadly speaking, white wines are of three types: Rhine wine, very light; sauterne, with heavier "bouquet," and not quite so sweet as the third, Chablis.

Red wines are clarets of the Bordeaux type, or Burgundies. Clarets are lighter in color, more tart, usually drier than Burgundies, and not so heady.

There are hundreds of brand names for wines, but in

nearly every country where grapes are grown commercially you'll find the same classifications. Thus there are American, French, Chilean, and other sauternes, Burgundies, and clarets. French wines are considered best, but there are plenty of excellent American ones too, and usually domestic sorts are cheaper than imports.

According to the experts, the ideal temperature for storing wines is 55° to 60° F. Since this is hardly possible in most homes, it is wise to buy only a few bottles at a time and store them in the coolest, darkest spot available—sunlight being another enemy. A shelf put up in the basement, downstairs hall, or bedroom, an old-fashioned wardrobe or kitchen "safe," all make satisfactory "cellars."

Where both white and red wines are on a menu, protocol requires the white be served first. Thus:

White ere red, steady head,
Red ere white, one hell of a night.

Red wine is served at room temperature. White wine is usually chilled, but avoid frosting or the bouquet will be lost.

FORTIFIED AND STILL WINES

The alcoholic content of wines varies from 9 to 14 per cent. Sherry, Marsala, Madeira, and port are fortified wines, because their alcoholic content has been raised from 16 to 23 per cent, often by the addition of brandy. Both red and white wines and fortified wines are known as *still* wines.

Sparkling Wines

Champagne and sparkling Burgundy are the two you are most likely to meet. Like red and white wines, alcoholic content varies from 9 to 14 per cent.

COOKING WITH WINE

When wines or spirits are cooked, the alcoholic content either disappears or is greatly reduced—only the flavor remains. Whenever possible, add liquor *after* food has been taken from the stove.

DINING WITH WINE AND SPIRITS

Want to know what the authorities say about which wines to serve with special courses and foods? Begin with the appetizer wines. Dry sherry heads the list, with Madeira for those who prefer something sweeter. If your choice runs to aromatic wines, you couldn't do better than vermouth, plain or mixed, chilled or blended with crushed ice. This much-neglected wine not only makes a fine apéritif, but has great value as a flavoring agent. Small wonder when we consider it contains "200 herbs, barks, flowers, seeds, peels, and leaves—ranging from allspice to zedoary root." (Zedoary, tab that one for your next game of Scrabble or anagrams.)

Champagne is wonderful at any time. It is proper to serve it before the meal, with the main course, or with dessert.

White wine is the accepted escort for shellfish, game birds, and white meat of poultry. Dark meat, game, roasts, and the like, have for years been served with red vintages. Soups, which have been flavored with fortified wines, are assigned the same partners. With cheese and nuts, port or Madeira are good companions. Pass something a little stronger with after-dinner coffee—brandy or a liqueur. If your guests want a drink after the meal, brandy is recommended.

HARD LIQUORS

And what about "hard" liquors? Your selection will vary according to your taste and that of your friends. In some places, bourbon is the preferred whisky; in others, Scotch or rye. If whisky seems expensive for cooking, substitute a domestic brandy such as applejack, distilled from apples, or kirsch, from cherries and originally Swiss, now produced in the United States. Kirsch, much used in cooking, is an important ingredient in cheese fondues, fruit compotes, or as an infusion with after-dinner coffee.

There are two types of rum: light, such as Bacardi from Cuba and Puerto Rico; dark and heavier, more full-bodied, from Jamaica and Trinidad. The heavier rums lend distinction to Planter's Punch, frozen Roman Punch, or Rum Cake, Nesselrode Pudding, and many other desserts.

Gin is, of course, the main ingredient in a Martini, Tom Collins, and many mixed drinks. It is also important in cooking, especially in marinades for certain oriental and exotic foods.

FIRST PURCHASES

Here's my list for your small shelf of household wines and spirits. Through this book you'll find numerous ways to use them as drinks or in recipes.

Bottle of white wine
Bottle of red wine
Bottle of light or dark rum or both
Bottle of fortified wine
Bottle of whisky
Bottle of cooking brandy
Bottle of gin
Bottle of dry vermouth
Bottle of sweet vermouth

LIQUEURS OR CORDIALS

Liqueurs, sometimes called cordials, are sweet sirups in assorted flavors, well spiked with strong spirits. Their number is legion, but here are a few of the best-known varieties which are also fine for flavoring.

Crème de Menthe—white and green—a delightful peppermint liqueur and a fine aid to digestion after a heavy meal. Often served frappéed over crushed ice.

Cointreau, Grand Marnier, Triple Sec, Curaçao—all variations of orange, the first two being French imports are expensive.

Drambuie—Scotch whisky blended with heather honey by a secret process.

Bénédictine (D.O.M.)—made by the Benedictine monks since the sixteenth century, and one of the finest of all liqueurs; also B. & B. (Bénédictine and Brandy).

Crème de Cacao—a happy marriage of vanilla and chocolate, is the main ingredient of Alexander cocktails, and an excellent addition to the kitchen shelf of flavorings.

3 SEASON TO TASTE

"The Magazine of Taste" was the name given a section in *The Cook's Oracle,* an early scientific cooking manual published in English. It referred to a cabinet where condiments and cooking aids were stored in the days before these items were commercially prepared. The author, Dr. William Kitchiner, was a London physician, man-about-town, amateur musician, epicure, and famous host. Accurate as a chemist's formula, his "receipts" for herb and spice powders, sauce enhancers, flavorings, essences, and salad vinegars are as valuable today as they were in 1817.

If you would like to try some of the good doctor's seasoning Rx.'s, here are a few I heartily recommend. They are a sure tonic for weak and ailing soups, sauces and gravies, a refresher for bland and listless salads.

Note: The special seasonings which follow are starred when used in recipes.

Browning

Place 1 cup sugar in a metal skillet. Turn heat high at first. Stir constantly. When lumps form, lower heat. Keep stirring, preferably with a wooden spoon, until lumps disappear. Quickly pour in ½ cup water—sugar will make a solid lump but no matter; in a moment it will dissolve leaving a thin, clear, brown liquid, a little darker and the same consistency as maple sirup. Remove from the stove; add 2 tablespoons salt. Stir until dissolved. Chill and bottle.

To use: Add ½ teaspoon Browning to 1 cup gravy, or 1 to 2 teaspoons put into soup will darken the color and improve the flavor.

"Made" Mustard (English Mustard)

This is one of the best-known recipes in *The Cook's Oracle.* Here is my adaptation of the original:

1 tablespoon dry mustard
1 tablespoon horse-radish vinegar (from prepared horse-radish)
1 tablespoon thick sour cream
1 teaspoon juice from grated onion
1 tablespoon cider vinegar (about)

Place mustard in a small bowl. Mix liquid ingredients, add slowly to mustard, and stir until well blended. Add enough cider vinegar to "thin to the consistency of a pap." Store in covered jars for use in salads or sauces, or with meats. It also adds a wonderful flavor to stuffed eggs.

Kitchen Spice (Ragout Powder)

2 tablespoons salt
1 tablespoon dry mustard
2 teaspoons allspice
2 teaspoons nutmeg
2 to 3 teaspoons black pepper
1 to 2 teaspoons cayenne or red pepper
2 teaspoons ginger
1 tablespoon dried lemon peel

Sift all ingredients except lemon peel. Prepare as below, add, and mix again. Store in a jar with a tight lid.

To prepare lemon peel: Grate the yellow part only; spread out on a cooky sheet or pie pan. Dry in a hot, dry place, then crumble into bits. Or rub the lemon peel on a lump of sugar until the oils have been incorporated. Dry the sugar and pound, then add to mix.

To use: Rub Kitchen Spice on roasts, as lamb or veal, spareribs, veal cutlets, or any other meat you want highly seasoned. Allow 2 to 3 teaspoons for a 4- to 6-pound roast, 1/4 teaspoon for a 1- to 1 1/2-pound cutlet. Add a teaspoon to a large pot of soup when meat is used. For meat or vegetable sauce, use 1/4 teaspoon to 1 cup gravy. This Kitchen Spice is delicious combined with a teaspoon of the Special Herb Mix which follows.

Special Herb Mix

2 ounces dried parsley
2 ounces dried winter savory
1 ounce dried lemon peel (as for Kitchen Spice above)
2 ounces dried sweet marjoram
2 ounces dried thyme
1 ounce dried sweet basil
1 teaspoon celery seed or celery salt
6 bay leaves

Pound ingredients in a mortar or crumble to blend. Store in jars with tight lids.

To use: Allow 1 teaspoon for a pot of soup, 1/4 to 1/2 teaspoon for 1 cup gravy or in a stew.

Note: A little postage scales makes a fine kitchen scales too.

Herb Vinegars

Weigh and wash 1 ounce of any fresh herb leaves—basil, mint, thyme, tarragon, etc. Put into a quart jar. Pack down and bruise with the back of a spoon. Fill up with white wine vinegar or cider vinegar. Cap tightly. Let stand for 10 days. Shake jar every day. Then strain through flannel or several thicknesses of cheesecloth or a linen napkin. Bottle and seal again.

To use: Add a little in sauces and salad dressings. To use mint vinegar with lamb, add sugar, salt, and pepper to taste. Make up just enough for each serving. Or add a tablespoon of the mint vinegar to peas just before serving.

Shallot, Garlic, or Onion Vinegar

Put 2 ounces (about 4 tablespoons) peeled, sliced shallots, garlic, or onions in a jar with about 1 quart of white wine vinegar. Cover, and allow to steep for 10 days. Shake container daily. Then strain off liquid into bottles. Cork and store.

To use: Add with a light hand. "A few drops will give a pint of gravy a sufficient smack of the garlic (or onion), the flavor of which, when slight and well-blended, is one of the finest we have; when used in excess, it is most offensive."

Chili Vinegar, Chili Wine

Steep 50 bird peppers or tiny chilies, cut in half or pounded, in 1 pint of wine vinegar or white wine for 2 weeks. Then strain and bottle.

To use: Whenever a recipe calls for vinegar plus pepper, or wine plus red pepper.

Thus endeth Dr. Kitchiner's lesson. Now to mine.

Sensation Seasoner

Here is a seasoning salt I like so much I keep it on the shelf beside my salt-and-pepper shakers. Many of my recipes call for it. (The amounts given for the salts are the sizes in which they are commercially bottled.)

2 ounces celery salt
2 ounces garlic salt
2 ounces onion salt
1 teaspoon black pepper
½ teaspoon cayenne or red pepper
1 tablespoon bright red paprika
1 tablespoon bright red chili powder

Sift ingredients together 3 times, and mix well. Place in jars or bottles with tight lids. To avoid solidifying, store in a cool, dry spot away from steam.

To use: Dust over poultry, meat, or fish. Then reduce by half the amount of ordinary salt. Allow about ¼ teaspoon Sensation Seasoner to 1 cup gravy, 1 teaspoon to a pot of soup, 1 tablespoon to a roast. Specific amounts will be given in the recipes.

A word of caution—avoid using Sensation Seasoner in more than one dish at a meal, as it has a distinctive flavor.

Monosodium Glutimate (M.S.G.)

This delightful seasoning aid, which looks like powdered sugar, brings out the flavor of cooked foods. I will simply refer to it as M.S.G. in the recipes.

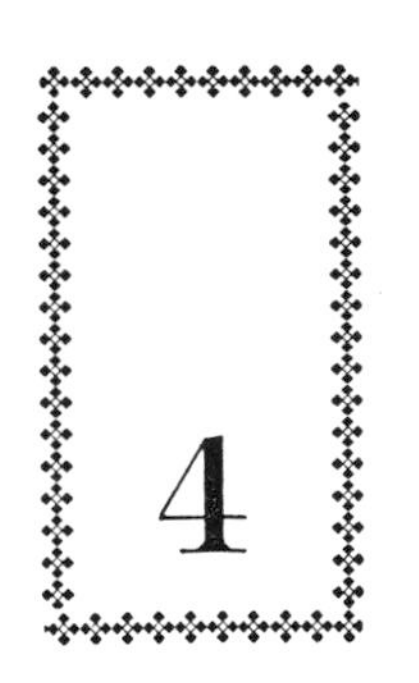

4 ALL AMERICAN

GREETINGS FROM DIXIE

CONCH COOKING, FLORIDA KEYS

Daiquiris with Key Limes

Cold Shrimp *Pickwick Café Sea-Food Dip* *

Arroz con Pollo * *(Spanish Chicken with Saffron Rice)*
surrounded by
Tiny Artichokes (canned)
Green Peas with Sesame-Seed Butter *
(in paper muffin cups)

Pickled Peaches *Hot Buttered Hard-Water Rolls*
Minted Melon Balls * *Iced Tea*

Accent Creole, New Orleans

New Orleans Gin Fizzes
Chicken Liver Pâté Mold * *Melba Toast Rounds*

Dixie Sea-Food Gumbo * *Rice* *French Bread* *Butterballs*
Heads of French Endive *Traditional French Dressing* *

Foolproof Biscuit Tortoni * *in Chocolate Cases* *
Demitasse *Crème de Menthe Frappé*

Cradle of the Confederacy, Alabama

Bourbon Old Fashioneds *Pippin Puffs* *

Old-Time Southern Barbecued Pork *
Alabama Succotash * *Ante-Bellum Combination Salad* *
Buttered Beaten Biscuits

Sherry-and-Brandy Jelly * *English Cream* * *Hot Coffee*

Bourbon Highballs *Deviled Pecans* *

Pickwick Café Crab Meat Gratin * *Potato Chips*
Old-fashioned Slaw *Buttered Brown-and-Serve Biscuits*

Mother's Nesselrode Pudding * *Hot Coffee*

Derby Winners, Kentucky

*Beforehand Mint Juleps * Chicken Livers in Bacon Jackets **

*Aspic of Beef Roularde, Duxelle **
*Triple Cheese-stuffed Potatoes **
*Green Beans and Eggplant, Hartnett **
Buttered Brown-and-Serve Rolls

*Heirloom Chess Tarts **
Hot Coffee

Kentucky Whisky Toddies
Fractured Franks (Sautéed Cocktail Sausages) *Pride-of-the-Bluegrass Mustard **

*Garibaldi Supper Salad **
Hot Buttered Poppy-Seed Bread

*Robert E. Lee Cake **
Iced Tea *Lemon* *Mint Sprigs*

Eastern Shore, Maryland Side

Bourbon-on-the-Rocks

Oyster Bar *Cocktail Sauces and Crackers*

Baltimore Crab Imperial *

Green Asparagus, Vinaigrette * *French-fried Potatoes* (frozen)

Baltimore Hard-Water Rolls,
Onion and Poppy-Seed Topping

Maryland Frozen Pudding
Orange Chiffon Cake (bought)
with Orange Cordial Frosting *
Hot Coffee

Eastern Shore, Virginia Side

President Madison's Whisky Sours *
Broiled Bacon-wrapped Stuffed Olives on Picks

Tidewater Chicken-and-Sweetbread Croquettes *
Brown Sherry Sauce *
Clover Leaf Rolls *Sweet Butter*
Cream O' Corn * *Sautéed Okra and Tomatoes*

Crème Brulée * *Cardinal Peaches* *
Demitasse

STERN ROCKBOUND COAST, NEW ENGLAND

Boston, Saturday Night

Hot Buttered Rum *New England Codfish Balls* *

Pickled Tongue in Mushroom-Wine Sauce *
Oven-baked Beans *Buttered Brown Bread*
Mustard Pickles

Boston Cream Cake * *with* *Jiffy Fudge Frosting* *
Hot Coffee

Down Easterners, Maine

Rock-and-Rye *Cheesy Popcorn* *

Cold Boiled Lobster in Shells *Green Mayonnaise* *
Mix-Your-Own Baked Potato served with
Butter *Sour Cream* *Chopped Chives*
Salt *Sensation Seasoner* * *Pepper Mill*
Old-fashioned Crunchy Cucumber Chips * *Sweet Gherkins*

Spiced Fruit in Wine *
Iced Tea with Lemon

Manhattan Medley

Manhattan Cocktails
Steak Tartare * *Toast Points*

Grand Central Station Oyster Bar Stew * *Oyster Crackers*
Mixed Green Salad *Garlic Dressing* *

Hot Fruit Compote * *Macaroons*
Hot Coffee

Fabulous Philadelphia

Rye Old Fashioneds *Crab-Meat Canapés*

Philadelphia Pepper Pot * *Hot Buttered Whole-Wheat Rolls*
Cucumber-stuffed Tomatoes with Water-Cress Dressing *

Strawberry Dream Cake *
Hot Tea

California Here We Come

Moscow Mules
(Vodka and Ginger Beer)
Cracked Crabs *Golden Gate Cocktail Sauce* *

Breasts of Chicken with Sour-Cream-and-Mushroom Sauce *
Caraway-Seed Bread Sticks *Chestnut Whip* *
Caesar Salad

Fresh Pineapple in Crème de Menthe
Hot Coffee

Zombie Cocktails
Mixed Salted Nuts *Cheese Crackers* *Cereal Bits*

Chilled Columbia River Salmon Steaks *
Caper Mayonnaise *
Poppy-Seed Rolls *Butter* *Shoestring Potatoes*
Combination Salad *Green Goddess Dressing* *

Orange Curd Tarts *
Hot Tea with Lemon

Tropical Paradise, Territory of Hawaii

Sleeping Giant Cocktails *
Salted Macadamia Nuts

Teriyaki Steak, Honolulu * *Korean Pepper Cabbage*
Chinese Fried Rice * *French Bread with Garlic Butter*
Herbed Cucumber-and-Onion Salad

Watermelon Shells with Tropical Fruit Cup *
Iced Tea Island Limes

Cane Cutter Cooler *
Arare
(Japanese Soy Crackers)

Madras Curried Spring Chickens *
Hawaiian Pineapple Pickle *
Rice Ring * *with Green Peas, Chinese Style* *
Split Buttered Hard-Water Rolls, Toasted

Honolulu Coconut Custard Pie
Hot Coffee

WHEN THE TOURIST RETURNS

NORTH CAPE CRUISE

Swedish Smörgåsbord

Aquavit

Swedish Meat Balls in Gravy * *Roast Beef*
Swedish Brown Beans *Mushroom Casserole*

Anchovies *Sardines* *Fish in Aspic* *Caviar*
Slivers of Smoked Salmon with Lemon
Cold Boiled Lobster with Mayonnaise *
Swedish Herring in Brine-and-Wine Sauces
Dilled Cucumbers in Marinade *Swedish Herring Salad* *
Potato Salad *Apple Salad*
Scandinavian Spiced Beets * *Stuffed Eggs* *Relishes*

Toasted Split Water Biscuits *Rye Bread with Caraway Seeds*
Rye Crisps *Swedish Limpa* *Whipped Butter*

Swedish Spiced Dried Fruit Soup * *Spritz Cookies*
Hot Coffee

DANISH DINNER

Brandy-and-Soda
Danish Open-faced Canapés of Smoked and Pickled Fish, Cheese, Cold Meats

Poached Lake Trout * *Lemon Sauce* *
Boiled Potatoes with Dilled Butter
Continental Bread *Danish Sweet Butter*
Red Raspberry Soup * *Cream*

Coffee
Cherry Heering

ERIN GO BAAA-AA-A

Irish Whisky-on-the-Rocks
Smoked Salmon Canapés

Sliced Cold Lamb with Chutney *Hard-Water Rolls*
Parslied Potato Salad *Minted Peas* *

Irish Lemon Curd Tarts *
Gaelic Coffee *

High Time for High Tea

Pimm's Cup No. 1: Bath Club, London *
English Cucumber-and-Potted-Prawn Sandwiches

Ham and Veal Pies * (hot or cold)
Broiled Tomato Halves *Chips (French Fries,* frozen)

English Cold Shape * *Stewed Damson Plums* *
Hot Tea with Milk or Lemon

Pink Gin *
Stilton Cheese *English Water Biscuits*

Regency Dandy's Oxtail Soup *
Cress-and-Tomato Salad served with
Cruets of Olive Oil and Malt Vinegar *Salt*
Freshly-ground Black Pepper
Buttered Toasted English Muffins *Wild Strawberry Jam*

Maids-of-Honor Tarts *
Hot Tea with Milk or Lemon
"A Dram of Drambuie"

Fashioned in France

Vermouth Cassis *
Anchovy-Cream-Cheese Spread * *in Toast Cases* *

Fillet of Beef, Flambé *
Potatoes Anna *Cold Artichokes with Poivrade Sauce* *
Hot Croissants *Sweet Butter Curls*

French Chocolate-Mocha Cream * *with Chantilly Crème*
(Vanilla-flavored Whipped Cream)
Demitasse
Grand Marnier

Dubonnet-on-the-Rocks with Lemon Peel
Alsatian Ham-and-Cheese Tartlets *

Cassoulet from Carcassonne *
Hot French Bread with Garlic Butter
Cucumbers in Vinaigrette Sauce * *on Chicory*
Chablis

Rice Imperial * *with 1830 Orange Compote* *
Demitasse
Cognac

Buono Appetito

Trocadero Vermouth Cocktail *

Antipasto * *Grissini (Italian Bread Sticks)*

Florentine Cannelloni with Cheese Sauce *

Chilled White Chianti

Mixed Salad Greens *Tarragon French Dressing* *

Italian Rum-and-Marron Cake *

Caffè Espresso

Strega

Martinis *Salted Filberts*

Melon and Prosciutto (Italian Ham)

Lasagne Zurla à la Leoni * *Italian Bread*

Red Chianti

Giacomoni's Vegetable Salad * *Neapolitan Dressing* *

Jellied Zabaglione * *Red Raspberry Purée* *

Caffè Espresso

Spanish Fandango

Manzanilla (Very Pale Light Sherry)
Salted Spanish Almonds *Spanish Green Olives*

Paella Valenciana *
Crusty Spanish Bread *Butter*

Caramel Flan * *Demitasse*
Anis Cordial

Madeira
Crisp Longostinas Fried in Glacé Batter
(Jumbo Shrimp)

Ragout of Lamb * *Saffron Rice* *
Spanish Green Salad * *Herbed Spanish Dressing* *
Buttered Seed Rolls

Spanish Almond Cake * *with Almond-Cocoa Frosting* *
Demitasse

Bahamian Buffet

Bimini Planter's Punch *
Cold Lobster Chunks on Picks *Garlic Mayonnaise* *

Seacrest Fish Chowder *
Sliced Buttered Home-Style Bread

Nassau Syllabub * *Coconut Cookies*
Iced Tea with Lime Slices

Scotch-and-Soda
Toasted Cheddar Cheese and Chutney Canapés

Lobster Tails in Bourbon Sauce *
Bahamian Peas and Rice *
Brussels Sprouts in Browned Butter
Split English Crumpets, Toasted and Buttered

Bakewell Tarts *
Hot Tea with Lemon

HUNGARIAN RHAPSODY

Maibowle * *Dilled Green Olives* *

Hungarian Lamb Roast with Sour Cream Gravy *
Red Cabbage, Sweet-and-Sour *
Buttered Noodles with Poppy Seeds
Vienna Rolls *Sweet Butter Balls*

Vanilla Mousse * *Hungarian Chocolate Torte*
Coffee
Tokay

6 MENUS ROUND THE CALENDAR

When Whistles Blow

Champagne Cocktails
Cold Shrimp on Picks *Sauce Ravigotte*

*Wednesday's Oysters * in Patty Shells* (bought)
New Potatoes (canned) *with Parsley Butter*
Buttered Brown-and-Serve Biscuits (frozen)
Orange, Grapefruit, Avocado on Boston Lettuce
*Vermouth Dressing **

*French Mocha-Praline Cake ** *Hot Coffee*

*Mulled Wine ** *Curried Peanuts ** *Sherried Olives **

*Sweetbread Vichyssoise **
*Sweetbread Hash * in Cheese-Noodle Ring **
Vegetable Salad in Tomato Aspic on Bibb Lettuce Heads
*Whipped Cream and Horse-Radish Mayonnaise **
Split Buttered Seed Buns

*Fruit Flambé ** *Hot Coffee*

Wind from the North

Hot Tom and Jerrys *Ham Salad Fingers* *

Shrimp, Ann Jeffries * *Rice Ring* *
Rye Rolls with Caraway Seeds
Deviled Cheese Aspic * *with Winter Fruit Salad*
(Tangerines, Oranges, Grapefruit, Apples,
Fresh Mushroom Slivers)

Hawaiian Pineapple-and-Ginger Dressing *
Hot Coffee
Bénédictine and Brandy

Hot Toddies
Bacon Spirals *

Veal Scaloppine with Marsala-Olive Sauce *
Spinach à la Russe * *Grissini*

Pears in Port * *Cupcakes*
Demitasse

SPRING BEAUTIES

Bacardi Cocktails
Raw Relishes with a Salt-filled Green Pepper for Dipping

*Coquilles Saint-Jacques * (Scallops in Shells) with*
Mashed Potatoes Piped Around the Edges
*Water Chestnuts and Peas in Bouillon *   Buttered Brioche*

*Cheese Tarts Royal, 1510 **
Demitasse

*Martinique Punch *   Curried Potato Chips **

*Chicken Abbott **
Noodles with Caraway Seeds
*Chef's Salad, Louisville **
*Roquefort or Danish Bleu Dressing **
Hot Buttered Beaten Biscuits

*French Strawberry Pudding **
Hot Coffee

Ninety in the Shade

Help-Yourself Supper

Iced Tea Iced Coffee Soft Drinks Cold Beer
Setups for Gin and Rum Drinks

Beef Tenderloin Corned Beef Ham Salami Bologna Sausage

Prepared Mustard Chili Sauce Sweet Pickle Relish
Prepared Horse-Radish
Old-fashioned Crunchy Cucumber Pickles *
Pickled Green Peppers * *Dill Pickles*

Split Buttered Baker's Buns Toasted Cross Crackers
Buttered Slices of Rye and Whole-Wheat Bread
Soda Crackers

Cheddar Swiss Camembert Danish Bleu Muenster Gruyère

Lettuce Endive Water Cress Romaine
Sliced Tomatoes Radish Roses
Marinated Cucumbers and Onions
Zucchini à la Grecque *
Slices of Peaches Pears Pineapple Cantaloupe Honeydew
Traditional French Dressing *
Roquefort and Danish Bleu Dressing *

Raspberry Sherbet in Cones Peach Ice Cream in Cones
Fudgies *

*Claret Cup **
*Curried Popcorn **

*Spiced Jellied Chicken Soup **
*Chicken Salmagundi **
Whole-Wheat Rolls *Butter*

Cantaloupe Halves with a Scoop of Vanilla Ice Cream
Iced Tea with Lemon

Rum Collins
Assorted Cocktail Crackers

*Whipped Salmon Mousse * on Shredded Lettuce with Quartered Hard-cooked Eggs and Peeled Tomatoes*
*Garlic Mayonnaise **
*Savory Stuffed Cymlings **
Toasted English Muffins, Buttered

*Tipsy Melon **
Frosted Spiced Tea with Lemon

For the Outdoor Grill

Gin-and-Tonic
Salted Cashew Nuts

Kentucky Grilled Steak with Henry Bane Sauce *
Plantation Potato Salad * *Baked Zucchini, Siena* *
Hot Buttered Brown-and-Serve Pocketbook Rolls

Snow Grapes *
Iced Tea with Lime Slices

Confederate Thanksgiving, circa 1864

Confederate Punch *
Salted Peanuts *Parched Corn*

War-Between-the-States Soup *
Beaten Biscuits *Butter*

Sherried Charlotte Russe *
Peach Brandy

Thanksgiving Today

Regent's Punch *
Cossack's Delight * *in Toast Cases* *

Broiled Smothered Turkey *
(Mock Pheasant)

Southern Grits Bread * *Wild Plum Jelly*
Broccoli in Vinaigrette Sauce *
Buttered Brown-and-Serve French Bread

Easy Rum Baba *
Hot Coffee

Christmas Gif'

Champagne Cocktail
*Caviar-frosted Cheese Mold * Toast Cases **

*Ham Baked in Ginger Ale * Pineapple-Cider-Raisin Sauce **
Chili Beans
*Bibb Lettuce Heads Henry Bane Dressing **
Buttered Brown-and-Serve Sesame-Seed Rolls

*Bond Family Dessert Eggnog **
Hot Coffee
Crème de Cacao

*Hot Winter Wassail **
*Liver Sausage in Sherried Aspic * Melba Toast*

*Roast Goose * Barley **
*Old-South Brandied Peaches **
*Sauerkraut in Wine with Caraway Seeds **
Hot Buttered Rye Bread
Sparkling Burgundy

*Bisque Ice Cream Fruit Flambé **
Demitasse

FRUGAL ELEGANCE

The fair, who's wise and oft consults our book,
And thence directions gives her prudent cook,
With choicest viands has her table crown'd,
And health, with frugal elegance is found.

—The Art of Cookery Made Plain and Easy
by Hannah Glasse, 1747

Budget Balancers

Alabama Sauterne Punch *
Tiny Ham Salad Roll-Ups *

Thick Vegetable Soup *
Hot Buttered Sesame-Seed Bread   *Grape Jelly*

Iced Coffee with a Scoop of Coffee Ice Cream
Melon Ka-Bobs *

Peachbowle *
Curried Potato Chips *

Turkey Hodgepodge * *on a Mound of Fluffy Rice*
Brown-and-Serve French Bread   *Butter*
Plantation Cabbage Salad *

Italian Cheese Custard *
Hot Coffee

Budget Balancers

Gay Nineties Claret Punch *
Cheese Straws

Noodles and Sausage, the Spanish Way *
Brown-and-Serve Rolls
Stuffed Pears (canned) *on Boston Lettuce*
(Cottage Cheese and Peeled Seeded Grapes)
Tarragon French Dressing *

My Apple Tarts *
Hot Chocolate

Sherry Flip
Fritos *Processed Bacon Rinds*

Stuffed Tufoli *
Quartered Iceberg Lettuce *Seneca Dressing* *
Buttered Poppy-Seed Rolls

Chocolate-Pecan Refrigerator Pudding *
Hot Coffee

The Tray's the Thing

Broom Sedge Cocktail *
Cocktail Ka-Bobs of Pickles, Pickled Onions, Cheese, Olives

Deep-South Barbecue for Buns *
Split Buns
Hogdenville Hot Pot * *Russian Sauerkraut Salad* *

Winter Compote * *Chocolate Nut Cookies*
Hot Coffee

Cinzano-on-the-Rocks with Lemon Peel
Chili con Guesso * *Split Toasted Cross Crackers*
(Cheese Dip)

Chicken Terrapin * *Parsley Rice* *
Green Bean Salad * *Herb Dressing* *
Toasted Hard-Water Rolls, Split and Buttered

Baked-Apple Meringues *
Hot Coffee

7 HERE'S HOW

Let's face it. We tend to serve the same drinks over and over again, even though we wouldn't dream of confronting the same people with the same menu each time they came to dine. Since there are so many exciting members of the cocktail family at large, it seems a shame not to invite them into our homes.

If your guests *insist* on their before-dinner Martinis, highballs, or old fashioneds, you have no choice but to serve what they prefer. But for those with imagination and adventurous tastes, you might offer one of the punches, cocktails, or other mixed drinks in this chapter. Here are recipes of some I've enjoyed as I sampled them traveling around.

Bartenders, take notice:

A jigger in any recipe in this chapter equals 1 ounce or 2 tablespoons; a bottle, 1/5 of a gallon or 3 1/5 cups.

READY-MIXED DRINKS

Beforehand Mint Juleps (About 12)

It's generally believed in Kentucky that the best mint juleps are mixed at the last moment, one at a time for each guest. But when you must serve a large group, this isn't always possible. Here's a formula I once devised when necessity demanded. Confidentially, no one seemed the wiser.

1 cup water
Few grains salt
1 cup sugar
1 large bunch mint sprigs tied together
1½ cups finely-chopped mint leaves
1½ to 2 jiggers aged bourbon whisky per julep
Extra mint sprigs

Boil water, salt, sugar and bunch of mint for 4 or 5 minutes or until mint turns brown. Put chopped mint in a bowl. Remove the bunch of mint and pour hot sirup over the fresh mint. Let stand until cool. Strain into a jar, cover, and refrigerate 2 or 3 days.

When ready to mix the juleps, chill cups or small highball glasses. Put in each a few tablespoons crushed ice, 1 tablespoon mint sirup, then add 1½ to 2 jiggers bourbon. Stir and taste. If not sweet enough, add more sirup. Stir again. Fill up the glasses with crushed ice. Tuck a tiny bunch of fresh mint sprigs in each glass and 2 straws cut the same height as the mint. It should be inhaled as the drink is sipped.

Frost the juleps in the refrigerator an hour or so before serving. Don't let your fingers touch the sides of the silver cup or glass. The prints show through the frosting.

President Madison's Whisky Sours (1 quart or 8 servings)

I came across this recipe in an old Virginia cookbook. These are supposed to be the whisky sours often served at the White House in Dolly Madison's day. They are definitely delicious—every bit as good as mixed at the last moment.

½ pint water
⅓ cup sugar (about)
4 lemons, juice and rinds
1 pint aged bourbon whisky (100 proof)

Boil water, sugar, and lemon rinds 3 minutes. Cool. Add lemon juice and bourbon. Taste, adding a little more sugar if needed, and refrigerate at least 12 hours. Remove rinds and squeeze dry. Strain and bottle.

FLOWING BOWL

A little water to make it weak,
A little sugar to make it sweet,
A little lemon to make it sour,
A little whisky to give it power.

Maibowle (8 servings)

This unusually refreshing drink comes from Hungary where fresh woodruff blooms in May. Dried woodruff is available in this country and there is a woodruff-flavored wine on the market. To prepare your own: Place 1½ to 2 tablespoons dried woodruff in a cheesecloth bag and drop into a bowl. Pour a bottle of white wine over the herb, cover, and let stand about 24 hours. Remove bag and strain.

1 bottle woodruff-scented wine
Block of ice
1 pint fresh strawberries
2 tablespoons sugar
1 tablespoon lemon juice (optional)

Pour the wine over ice in your punch bowl. Add sweetened strawberries, and lemon juice if using it. Ladle back and forth until chilled.

Peachbowle

For each guest, allow one dead-ripe freestone peach (medium-sized). Peel the peaches and prick all over with a fork. Place in the punch bowl. Sprinkle with sugar, a tablespoon for each peach, and let stand 10 minutes. Pour chilled white wine or champagne over the peaches, one or two bottles, depending on the number of guests. Stir well before serving. If you expect the Peachbowle to stand a long time, place a block of ice in the bowl after adding the wine. Ladle back and forth occasionally to keep chilled.

Frosted Fruit for the Punch Bowl

People are really ingenious! Recently I read an article on frosting whole, fresh fruits—bunches of grapes, cherries, plums, nectarines, peaches, pears, and whatever else you wish. The process is simple: Put unwrapped, unpeeled fruit on a tray or piece of foil-covered cardboard in the freezer for about two hours, or until fruit is frozen hard. Remove to the punch bowl at once. As soon as the air strikes the fruit, it acquires a flattering coat of bloom. Use in place of ice. (The fruit should be eaten soon after it thaws as it is apt to soften and cannot be re-frozen.) For an elegant centerpiece, try Frosted Fruit in this punch:

Alabama Sauterne Punch (8 servings)

1 quart sauterne
Juice of 4 oranges
Juice of 4 lemons
Thin peeling of 1 small cucumber
1 cup pineapple juice
Sugar to taste

Mix all ingredients in a large bowl or pitcher with ice cubes. Refrigerate until thoroughly chilled. Pour in punch bowl filled with Frosted Fruit. Or use a pint of peeled, summer fruit, sweetened to taste, and a block of ice. Ladle back and forth until sufficiently chilled.

Regent's Punch (12 servings)

There is a story that the Prince Regent, later George IV of England, not only originated this punch, but consumed great quantities of it. This is an excellent wedding punch and is certainly at home on the buffet table, indoors or out.

1 cup strong black tea infusion
2 lemons, juice and rinds
¾ cup cognac
¾ cup Jamaica rum
¾ cup curaçao
Sugar to taste
1 quart champagne
Block of ice

Pour hot tea into a large bowl, add all other ingredients except champagne and ice. Chill overnight. Remove rinds. Strain into punch bowl over ice and pour in champagne. Ladle to mix well. (By *infusion* I mean brewed tea.)

Confederate Punch (36 to 40 servings)

This is said to have been a favorite of Jefferson Davis, President of the Confederacy during the Civil War. I hope it cheered him and the other valiant Southerners who gathered round his punch bowl. I know it will cheer you.

1 cup lemon juice
1 to 1½ cups sugar to taste
4 bottles claret
1 pint sherry
⅔ cup brandy
⅓ cup light rum
⅓ cup maraschino liqueur (not cherry juice)
2 thick slices cucumber with peel
2 lemons, sliced thin, seeds removed
1 orange sliced thin, seeds removed
1 bottle ginger ale
2 bottles sparkling water
Block of ice

Mix all ingredients except cucumber, fruit slices, ginger ale, ice, and sparkling water at least 24 hours before serving. This mellows the brew. Keep well covered but it is not necessary to refrigerate. Pour over block of ice in punch bowl. Add other ingredients, ladle back and forth until well blended and cold. Serve in punch cups.

Gay Nineties Claret Punch (25 servings)

This is my mother's recipe, and very good it is, too!

2½ quarts claret
1 pint strong tea infusion
½ cup Jamaica rum
Juice of 12 lemons
No. 2½ can pineapple chunks (and juice)
1 cup sugar or more
Block of ice
½ pint drained maraschino cherries or fresh cherries
Long thin strip of cucumber peeling
1 quart sparkling water

Mix claret with the brewed tea (my mother used a black- and orange-pekoe mixture). Add rum, lemon and pineapple juice, and sugar to taste. This can be mixed the day before it is used. When ready to serve, place ice in punch bowl, put in all the fruits and green peel. Add sparkling water to liquids and pour over ice. Ladle back and forth until cold. Serve in punch cups.

Claret Cup (12 servings)

A delightful drink on a hot day.

1 bottle Bordeaux Red or claret
2 ounces port
2 ounces curaçao or other orange liqueur
Juice of 1 lemon
1 bottle sparkling water
1 pint fresh strawberries
Sugar
Block of ice

Stir together all ingredients except the strawberries and sugar. Cut berries in half, mix with ¼ to ½ cup sugar, and let stand until sugar dissolves, 10 to 20 minutes. Then add to claret mixture. Add more sugar if necessary. Chill until ready to serve. Pour into the punch bowl over ice. Ladle back and forth to make punch very cold.

Mulled Wine (About 40 servings)

This tastes so good on a cold winter night—and especially on New Year's Eve.

1 cup water
1 cup sugar
3 quarts red wine
2 quarts water
6 sticks cinnamon
2 or 3 pieces dried ginger root
2 blades mace
2 tablespoons whole allspice
1 tablespoon whole cloves
1 tablespoon whole coriander or cardamom seeds
¼ teaspoon freshly-grated nutmeg
3 lemons, juice and rinds
¼ bottle mild rum or arrack
Extra stick cinnamon to use as straws

The day before: Boil the cup of water with sugar for 5 minutes. Set aside. Pour wine into a large kettle, add the 2 quarts water, the whole spices, tied in a cheesecloth bag (large enough to let them expand), nutmeg, lemon juice, and rinds. Bring mixture to a hard boil, turn off heat, cover, and let steep. Do not remove spices until mixture cools to room temperature. Pour into bottles or jars with lids. If made several days ahead, refrigerate.

When ready to serve, heat the spiced wine to boiling. Remove from stove, add rum, or arrack if you can find it. Serve in Tom-and-Jerry mugs with handles. Place stick cinnamon or straws in each mug.

Hot Winter Wassail (32 servings)

Nothing warms the cockles of the heart like a hot, spicy wassail! In Georgian England, it was traditional to offer this to the young people, who, at Christmastime, made the neighborhood rounds, singing carols and putting on the play of *St. George and the Dragon*. It is one of the most inexpensive drinks I know—and one of the most delicious.

1 gallon apple cider
1 tablespoon whole cloves
1 tablespoon whole allspice
2 sticks cinnamon (4 to 5 inches long)
2 blades mace
¼ teaspoon powdered ginger
¼ teaspoon grated nutmeg
¼ teaspoon salt
1 cup dark brown sugar (about)
1 pint gin or vodka
2 lemons, sliced thin, seeds removed
3 oranges, sliced thin, seeds removed

Pour cider into a large kettle, add spices and salt. Bring to a hard boil, then reduce heat, cover and simmer 15 minutes. Remove from stove, add sugar to taste if needed. Let wassail cool, then strain it. Keep in a cool place until ready to use, but it is not necessary to refrigerate. Near serving time, let spiced cider come to a boil. Pour into the wassail bowl.

To prepare the wassail bowl, use a heavy china bowl or crock or a silver punch bowl. Heat it over a large kettle of boiling water. Add lemon and orange slices. When warm, add gin or vodka and let it heat (but do not boil; spirits will evaporate). Pour in the boiling wassail. The pottery bowl can be placed over an alcohol burner if you wish. Ladle the wassail into cups and serve.

COCKTAILS

Broom Sedge Cocktail (12 servings)

Once when my husband and I were in Williamsburg, Kentucky, visiting a fabulous native son, the late Judge H. H. Tye, (also author of a local column, *Broom Sedge Philosophy*), the "Jedge's" wife served this cocktail. The guests all raved about it, but not the host. He insisted it didn't have enough "critter" in it. But there are occasions when you want a before-supper cocktail without too much kick. I recommend this one named for a wise and witty gentleman of the old school.

4 cocktail glasses orange juice
2 cocktail glasses grenadine
6 cocktail glasses gin
2 tablespoons heavy cream
Sugar to taste

Mix all ingredients and let mellow in the refrigerator until very cold. Chill the glasses and serving pitcher or cocktail shaker, stir or shake, and serve at once. If you are in a hurry you can chill this in a blender with 3 cubes of ice, crushed.

Sleeping Giant Cocktail (1 serving)

This cocktail from Kauai Inn on the Island of Kauai—most beautiful of all the Hawaiian group I think—is especially appropriate to serve on a very hot night.

1 ounce light rum
1 ounce gold rum
½ ounce lemon juice
½ ounce sugar sirup
3 or 4 chunks pineapple (fresh or canned)
1 green cherry
½ ounce light rum

Mix everything except fruit and extra ½-ounce light rum in a blender with a few cubes of crushed ice, or in a cocktail shaker. When very cold, pour into a brandy snifter. Add fruit. Spread light rum over top. Serve.

Trocadero Vermouth Cocktail (1 serving)

This cocktail is a delightful apéritif from the Trocadero Restaurant, The Hague, Holland.

1 jigger French vermouth
½ jigger Italian vermouth
Dash grenadine
Dash orange bitters
Thin slice lemon

Shake vermouth, grenadine, and bitters well with 2 ice cubes. Strain into the glass. Twist lemon slice and drop into the cocktail.

Vermouth Cassis (1 serving)

A very popular cocktail in France—where cocktails are usually frowned upon.

¾ ounce crème de cassis
1½ ounces French vermouth
Sparkling water

Pour crème de cassis (a French liqueur made from black currants) and vermouth into an 8-ounce highball glass containing 2 or 3 ice cubes. Add sparkling water to fill glass, stirring well. In France, this drink is often served in champagne glasses.

Pink Gin (1 serving)

Ever since it was circulated that this was the favorite before-dinner drink of Prince Philip, Consort of Queen Elizabeth II, it has been a popular cocktail. I think it's much more palatable than a Martini—but I'm not a gin drinker. Pour 1 to 1½ ounces gin over 3 ice cubes in an old-fashioned glass. Add 2 dashes Angostura bitters or enough to give a faint pink cast. Add water to fill glass. Muddle until cold.

COOLERS

Martinique Punch (1 serving)

This recipe is from the assistant purser on the *S.S. Liberté* in June 1951.

Crushed ice to fill a fruit juice glass
1 teaspoon thick Sugar Sirup or more (see recipe)
1 jigger Martinique or dark Jamaica rum
1 slice lime, unpeeled

Fill glass with ice. Combine other ingredients except lime and stir well. Pour into glass, add lime, and serve at once.

Bimini Planter's Punch (3 servings)

This recipe, concocted in the Bahamas, was the best Planter's Punch I ever drank. The original served this amount as one portion, but I think it's enough for three.

1 jigger Bacardi rum
2 jiggers Jamaica rum
1 jigger port
½ jigger Drambuie
2 cups pineapple juice (fresh or frozen)
Dash cinnamon
3 slices pineapple
3 slices orange, seeds removed
3 half-slices grapefruit, seeds removed

Whip all ingredients, except the fruit slices, in a blender, or shake 2 minutes in a cocktail shaker. In each glass (I use double old-fashioned glasses) place 4 cubes of ice and a slice of each fruit. Pour the punch over and serve.

Pimm's Cup No. 1: Bath Club, London (4 servings)

It was a memorable occasion when my friends, Edith and John Nitch-Smith, urged me to try this cooler at their London club. They persuaded the bartender to give me the directions for making this prized summer drink.

Please don't make it with soft drinks or synthetic citrus fruit juices. The base should be a good lemonade made from fresh or frozen lemons or limes.

6-ounce can frozen lemonade
3 cans (2¼ cups) water
6 ounces Pimm's Cup No. 1
4 thin slices orange, seeds removed
4 thin slices lemon, seeds removed
4 thin slices unpeeled cucumber
4 sprigs fresh mint or ¼ teaspoon dried

Mix lemonade and water in a blender or with a rotary beater. Add Pimm's Cup No. 1 and stir well. Fill 4 large highball or double old-fashioned glasses with 3 cubes of ice each. Put a slice of each fruit, cucumber, and mint sprig or pinch of dried in each. Pour in Pimm's Cup mixture. Stir until cold. And sip.

Cane Cutter Cooler (1 serving)

This refreshing cooler was a specialty of the charming Maui Palms Hotel, on the island of Maui, Hawaii.

1 jigger rum
½ ounce lemon juice
1 ounce orange juice
1 ounce pineapple juice
1 teaspoon sugar
Dash Angostura bitters
Slice of pineapple, orange, and a red cherry to garnish

Mix all ingredients except fruits in a cocktail shaker with a few cubes of ice. When well chilled, pour into a small highball glass. Fill with crushed ice, add fruit. Serve with straws.

AFTER-DINNER "SIPPAGE"

Gaelic Coffee (1 serving)

Jim Galvin presented me with this enchanting after-dinner drink at his Portmarnoch Country Club outside of Dublin. He and Mrs. Galvin (once the manager of Sacher's Hotel in Vienna) have now sold their club, but memories of the wonderful week my husband and I spent with them will always be treasured.

¾ cup boiling hot coffee
1 to 2 tablespoons sugar
1½ ounces aged Irish whisky
Heavy cream

Pour coffee into an 8-ounce glass. Add sugar to taste and stir until dissolved, then add whisky. Float cream on top until glass is full. *Don't stir.* Just sip, and let the cool cream temper the fiery coffee and whisky. If this is the food of the leprechauns, no wonder they can accomplish miracles!

8 COCKTAIL ASSOCIATES, LTD.

Select hors d'oeuvre which complement the other dishes on your menu. If a thick soup or a plain casserole is to be the main dish, serve a filling and rather elaborate hors d'oeuvre—Caviar-frosted Cheese Mold or sea food with a dip—and consider it the first course. If the dinner itself is quite rich, pass something light and simple—Sherried Olives or Curried Potato Chips. With a cold supper, offer a piping-hot tidbit; or a cold pick-up, when the rest of the food is hot.

COLD HORS D'OEUVRE

Antipasto (6 to 8 pints)

As devotees of Italian cooking well know, antipasto is the ideal first course when lasagne, spaghetti, tufoli, or other pasta is the main dish. With a 6-quart pressure cooker, it is as easy as vegetable soup; cooking and processing are reduced to a minimum. Otherwise, process by the open-kettle method as outlined in any standard cookbook.

1½ cups celery, cut in inch pieces
½ pound tender green beans
1 green pepper, slivered
2 carrots, scraped and sliced thin
2 cups peeled onions (whole little onions or large ones, sliced)
1 small cauliflower, separated into tiny flowerettes
2 cups water or more
2 cups peeled ripe tomatoes or drained canned ones
1½ teaspoon salt (about)
¼ teaspoon black pepper
1 bay leaf
2 cloves
¼ teaspoon basil or orégano
3 garlic cloves, minced

2 tablespoons cornstarch
1 cup cider vinegar
6-ounce can tomato paste
1 tablespoon sugar
1 cup olive oil or part salad oil, part oil drained from sea food
2 (6-ounce) cans button mushrooms or ½ pound fresh
½ cup stuffed olives
½ cup ripe olives, seeds removed
8- to 10-ounce can artichoke hearts, drained (optional)
19-ounce can tiny onions, drained (optional)
1 or 2 (6-ounce) cans tuna fish, drained
1 or 2 (2-ounce) cans anchovies, drained
1 or 2 (3¾-ounce) cans boned sardines, drained

Boil the left column of ingredients in the pressure cooker ½ minute at 15 pounds' pressure—a minute makes the vegetables a little soft. Open cooker according to manufacturer's directions. Drain vegetables, putting the liquid back in cooker. Put vegetables aside. Add cornstarch, mixed to a paste with a little vinegar, to the cooker. Stir in remaining vinegar, tomato paste, sugar, and all but 4 tablespoons oil. Let come to a boil, stirring constantly, preferably with a wooden spoon. Cook 2 minutes or until the consistency of a thin cream sauce. Add pressure-cooked vegetables, mushrooms, sautéed 5 minutes in the 4 tablespoons of oil, olives, the artichokes and extra onions if using them. Heat thoroughly but do not boil. Correct seasoning.

Divide sea food among 6 or 8 pint jars—if making the whole amount you will need 2 cans of each fish. *Fill jars to within 1 inch of the top* with the antipasto. Wipe and put on tops lightly. Do not screw tight. Stand jars on a trivet in the cooker. Do not let them touch; I can only prepare 4 jars at a time. Pour in 2 cups water and cook for 4 minutes at 10 pounds' pressure. Cool in cooker. Remove jars, tighten lids, wipe dry, and store.

To serve, place a jar of homemade antipasto in the center of a large platter lined with lettuce leaves. Surround with a selection of the following:

Hard-cooked eggs, halved and frosted with mayonnaise, garnished with chopped herbs—chives, parsley, basil, orégano—then placed on tomato slices.

Chilled Cucumbers in Vinegar Dressing

Italian Pickled Green Peppers

Italian Olives, Sardines, and Anchovies

Tuna Fish (canned), covered with thick sour cream and sprinkled with drained capers.

Prosciutto (Italian ham), Pepperoni (anise-flavored sausage) and Italian Salami, all sliced very thin.

This stretches a pint to serve about a dozen. But you can serve just the antipasto to 5 or 6 guests in individual portions on salad plates.

Steak Tartare (8 servings)

Diamond Jim Brady, whose voracious appetite caused headlines at the turn of the century, is said to have consumed fantastic amounts of Steak Tartare at after-theater suppers. It is an appropriate hors d'oeuvre today too, particularly when the rest of the meal is not too filling. Serve on a platter surrounded by thinly-sliced, buttered rye bread, or toast triangles. Have butter knives for spreading.

1 pound sirloin, tenderloin, or top round of prime beef
1 medium onion, peeled and grated
3 anchovies, mashed, or salt to taste
¼ teaspoon freshly-ground black pepper
1 egg yolk or enough to hold meat together
Extra anchovy curls for garnish
Chopped parsley for garnish

Get the best beef available. Have *all* fat removed and the lean part put through the grinder 3 times. Mix meat with other ingredients except garnishes. Form into a loaf shaped like a fat sausage. Crisscross top with the dull edge of a knife making squares or diamonds, and press an anchovy curl into each. Sprinkle with parsley. Wrap loaf in waxed paper and refrigerate until ready to serve.

Variation: If you and your guests are garlic fanciers, add an average-sized clove, crushed, with the other ingredients.

Chicken Liver Pâté Mold (8 to 12 servings)

12 chicken livers
4 tablespoons butter or chicken fat
2 tablespoons olive oil
2 onions, peeled and diced
¼ cup sour or sweet cream
Salt and pepper to taste
1 tablespoon Worcestershire sauce
¼ teaspoon soy sauce
¼ teaspoon Sensation Seasoner *
1 tablespoon gelatin
10½-ounce can (1¼ cups) bouillon
Hard-cooked egg, riced
Parsley or water cress

Sauté livers in melted fat for 5 minutes. Use a deep covered skillet and have heat low. They should be done through, but not browned. Turn once. If still pink inside, cook 3 to 5 minutes more. Remove livers, sauté onions in same pan until tender. Stir constantly. Combine with livers and excess fat. Put in a blender or, if you don't have one, grind through finest blade of the meat grinder. Add cream and seasonings.

Soften gelatin in ¼ cup cold bouillon. Set container over hot water and cook until gelatin melts. Then mix with rest of bouillon. Add to liver paste (if you used the grinder) or put in the blender and whip smooth. Correct seasoning and pour into a lightly-greased, pint-sized ring or fluted mold. Refrigerate until firm.

Unmold on a platter, sprinkle the egg over top, and surround with a wreath of parsley or water cress. Have Melba toast or toast triangles and butter knives nearby.

Liver Sausage in Sherried Aspic (8 servings)

1 small liver sausage
1 tablespoon gelatin
10½-ounce can bouillon
2 teaspoons Worcestershire sauce
¼ teaspoon soy sauce
*Dash each of M.S.G., Tabasco sauce, Sensation Seasoner * (or garlic salt)*
2 tablespoons sherry (about)

Peel sausage and set aside. Soften gelatin in ¼ cup cold bouillon; add remaining bouillon, then cook over hot water until gelatin melts. Stir in seasonings and sherry. Place in refrigerator.

When mixture begins to thicken, pour a little into a glass with straight sides—an iced tea or highball glass will do. Put sausage in the glass. (If it is too long, cut in half and use 2 glasses.) Pour on remaining aspic. Be sure sausage is *completely* surrounded. Refrigerate until firm.

To serve: Unmold, slice into ¼-inch rounds, and arrange on a platter with Melba toast. Rye bread or soda crackers are also delicious with this.

Variation: Try a 7-inch piece of large, peeled Milwaukee Braunschweiger instead of liver sausage. Use a loaf pan for the mold.

Caviar-frosted Cheese Mold (12 servings)

I first tasted this at Alice Grey's. She gave me the ingredients but could not remember the proportions. So I worked them out and this cheese mold tastes exactly like hers. It is the best way I know to make a small jar of caviar serve twelve people.

1 cup sour cream
1 cup creamed cottage cheese
1 clove garlic, crushed
1 teaspoon Worcestershire sauce
*¼ teaspoon Sensation Seasoner **
Dash soy sauce
Dash Tabasco
1 tablespoon gelatin
¼ cup sherry
4-ounce jar imported caviar
Juice of ½ lemon

Put sour cream, cottage cheese, garlic, and seasonings in a blender, or use an electric beater, and mix until lumps disappear. Soften gelatin in cold sherry; then place over hot water until gelatin melts. Add to cream-cheese mixture and whip again until light. Pour into a lightly-greased pint mold. (I used a fluted mold but a mixing bowl will do.) Put in refrigerator until firm. Allow at least 24 hours before using.

To serve: Unmold on a platter. Mix caviar with lemon juice and frost the cheese mold. Surround with unsalted crackers or Melba toast rounds.

Sea Food and Dips

The most satisfactory way I've found to serve boiled sea food and dips at a cocktail-supper is this: Fill a silver punch bowl or deep pottery bowl about two inches from the top with equal parts of crushed dry ice and regular ice. Put a smaller bowl in the center, firm the ice around it, and fill it with the sea-food dip. Shrimp, lobster tails cut in bite-sized pieces, crab claws, or other fish go right on the ice (speared with picks). Everything keeps well chilled for an hour or longer.

Pickwick Café Sea Food Dip (10 to 12 servings)

This sauce was created by Fred Rudolphi, whose Pickwick Café in Montgomery, Alabama, was known throughout the South. Here's the recipe as he gave it to my mother.

2 tablespoons tarragon vinegar
½ pint mayonnaise (homemade if possible; see recipe)
½ teaspoon Tabasco
1 teaspoon anchovy paste or 1 tablespoon minced anchovies (about)
½ pint chili sauce

Add vinegar to mayonnaise slowly, beating until smooth. Add Tabasco. Combine anchovy with a little of the mayonnaise mixture. Add remaining ingredients and more anchovy if not salty enough. Whip in a blender if handy. This should be enough for 2 to 3 pounds of sea food.

Golden Gate Cocktail Sauce (8 servings)

This popular West Coast dip masquerades under various names—usually in honor of a particular restaurant or hotel. It is a fine complement to all sorts of sea food.

1 cup chili sauce
¼ cup French dressing (made with wine vinegar, lemon juice, olive oil)
1 tablespoon prepared horseradish
1 tablespoon Worcestershire sauce
2 tablespoons minced green pepper
2 tablespoons minced parsley
2 tablespoons minced chives or green shallots with tops
2 tablespoons minced celery
Dash Tabasco
Salt and pepper to taste

Mix all the ingredients together. If too thick, add a little more French dressing.

Anchovy-Cream-Cheese Spread (8 servings)

2 (3-ounce) packages cream cheese
3 drops Tabasco
1 tablespoon French dressing or more
1 clove garlic, crushed
1 tablespoon anchovy paste or more

Mash softened cream cheese with a fork. Add Tabasco and French dressing making a smooth paste. Mix in garlic and anchovy paste. If too stiff, add more French dressing, but don't make it runny. Add more anchovy if not salty enough. Serve on crackers, Melba toast rounds or in Toast Cases (see recipe below).

HOT STUFF

Bacon Spirals

The first time I tasted one of these tantalizing swirls, I was stumped by the filling. Crisp bacon covered something crunchy—but what! After a brief inspection I had the answer —those long soda crackers known as Saratoga Flakes.

To prepare them, snap crackers along the dotted line. Wrap thin slices of breakfast bacon spirally around crackers, the edges overlapping, so core is completely covered. Secure at each end with picks. Bake for 20 to 30 minutes in an iron skillet in a 450° F. oven. They should be brown all over. Drain on absorbent paper and serve piping hot. You can get them ready for baking the morning of the party, but do not refrigerate. Bake at the last minute.

Cossack's Delight (8 servings)

I first encountered this mushroom-and-sour-cream dish years ago in New York, at the Russian Tea Room next to Carnegie Hall. Whether my approximation of the recipe has all the ingredients that the original did, I'll never know, but "it's sure good eatin'."

1 pound fresh mushrooms
1 large clove garlic, crushed
2 tablespoons butter or margarine
2 tablespoons olive oil
1 small onion, peeled and grated
1/8 teaspoon M.S.G.
1/8 teaspoon dry mustard
1/2 teaspoon soy sauce
1/8 teaspoon paprika
Salt and pepper to taste
1 tablespoon flour
1 cup sour cream

Wash mushrooms but do not peel. Place in a wooden bowl with garlic and chop very, very fine. Use a nut chopper if handy. Heat fat and olive oil in a Dutch oven. Add onion, juice and pulp. Let cook a minute, then mix in mushrooms. Cook 3 minutes, stirring constantly. Season, and add flour, mixed to a paste with a little cream, then blend in rest of cream. Turn heat low, stir until thickened and well heated. *Do not let boil.* Put on the buffet table in a chafing dish or food warmer and surround with Melba toast or Toast Cases (see recipe below).

Variation: A cup of minced, baked ham or chicken is delicious with this dish and helps stretch it.

Toast Cases

This is a really useful hors d'oeuvre recipe. The cases can be made days ahead, frozen, then reheated at the last minute.

Buy day-old bread and chill before slicing. If your baker will do it for you, tell him it should be about a quarter of an inch thick; otherwise slice bread as thin as you can. With a biscuit-cutter, cut out rounds to fit muffin pans. (Use the tiny pans for these cases.)

Fit rounds into pans, press into shape. The bread should come to the top of the sides as a piecrust does. Brush lightly with melted butter or margarine. Place pans in a 400° F. oven for 7 minutes, or until cases are golden brown. Don't let them burn. Fill with hot or cold spreads. And if cases have been chilled, reheat just before using.

Chili con Guesso (8 servings)

Virginia Kelly served this snappy-cheese dip at one of her cocktail parties. I was impressed with its piquant flavor, and the fact that it remained smooth all evening. The secret is to use Cheese Whiz. Here is her recipe:

1 large onion, peeled and grated
¼ cup butter
1 clove garlic, mashed, or ¼ teaspoon garlic powder
1 teaspoon chili powder or more to taste
10½-ounce can condensed tomato soup
½ pound Cheese Whiz or Velveeta cheese, cubed
1 teaspoon Worcestershire sauce
Salt
Tabasco or cayenne pepper

Sauté onion in melted butter in a chafing dish or heavy iron skillet. When soft and yellow, add garlic, chili powder, and tomato soup. Place in top of a double boiler if not using a chafing dish. Cook until mixture boils and is well blended. Then add cheese and Worcestershire sauce, and stir until cheese melts. Add seasonings to taste. Serve in a chafing dish or pottery casserole placed over a warmer. Toasted tortillas, cross crackers, or soda crackers are good with this.

Note: For tomato soup, you can substitute 1¼ cups tomato juice thickened with 1 tablespoon flour, and an extra teaspoon Worcestershire sauce.

Pippin Puffs (20 puffs)

Carita Ackerly gave me the recipe for these delectable, easy-to-make cheese cookies. They must be baked at the last minute and served piping hot, but the dough can be made up the day before and refrigerated until party time. It also freezes well.

1 cup sifted flour
3-ounce Pippin Cheese Roll
⅛ teaspoon dry mustard
¼ teaspoon nutmeg
¼ teaspoon salt
½ cup butter, softened

Blend all ingredients together as for piecrust. Work until dough holds together and looks like cooky dough. If too soft to handle, chill about 20 minutes in the refrigerator. Pinch off teaspoons of dough and roll into small balls. Place 2 inches apart on an ungreased cooky sheet and bake in a 375° F. oven, 10 to 15 minutes. Puffs should hold their shape when lifted, but do not bake till hard and brown. (Baking time is a little longer if dough has been refrigerated.) For smaller puffs, use a ½-teaspoon measure; these will be done in 5 to 8 minutes.

Variation: To make an attractive design, dip a four-pronged fork into bright red paprika, and press ridges in top of each cheese ball just before baking.

Ham Salad Fingers (12 servings)

Ham Salad

1 cup ground baked ham
1 tablespoon minced parsley
2 teaspoons pickle relish or French dressing
1 teaspoon grated onion
½ teaspoon dry mustard or 1 teaspoon prepared
1 teaspoon prepared horse-radish
¼ cup mayonnaise or sour cream
1 teaspoon Worcestershire sauce
Salt
Pepper

Combine all the ingredients but do not have mixture too runny. It should be just moist enough to hold together.

The Fingers: Half the English Paste recipe or any piecrust recipe using 2 cups flour will be adequate. Roll dough on a floured board to ⅛-inch thickness. Cut into 2- by 10-inch strips.

To make, pile Ham Salad ½ inch from one edge. Fold narrow edge of dough over filling, then with a spatula, fold over the wide edge, making a tight roll. Use a very sharp knife to cut into finger-length strips. Place on an ungreased cooky sheet, seam side down. Bake in a 450° F. oven for 10 to 12 minutes, or until crust browns. Serve at once.

You can make Ham Salad Fingers the day before, refrigerate, then bake just before serving. For variety, sprinkle a tablespoon of grated Parmesan cheese over the Ham Salad before rolling.

Tiny Ham Salad Roll-Ups (12 servings)

Instead of Ham Salad Fingers, roll the dough into thin 5- by 10-inch rectangles. Spread Ham Salad over center of each, leaving ½ inch bare all around it. Roll up like a jelly roll. Cut into ½-inch slices, place on an ungreased cooky sheet 2 inches apart, and bake as directed in the recipe above.

Alsatian Ham-and-Cheese Tartlets (18 to 20 tartlets)

There is always something fascinating about small things, and these minute tartlets are no exception. Use half the English Paste dough (see recipe in Tazza of Tasty Tarts) and either tartlet or small muffin pans. Line the pans with dough the day before they are to be served, and refrigerate. Add the filling the morning of the party. Bake just before serving.

½ to ⅓ cup ground baked ham
1 to 2 cups shredded Swiss cheese
2 tablespoons butter or olive oil
1 tablespoon grated onion
⅛ teaspoon M.S.G.
1 cup cream
1 teaspoon Worcestershire sauce or more
¼ teaspoon salt (about)
*⅛ teaspoon Sensation Seasoner * or seasoning salt*
⅛ teaspoon grated nutmeg
1 tablespoon flour
2 eggs
¼ cup grated Parmesan or Swiss cheese (about)

In the bottom of each dough-lined pan, place about 1 teaspoon of ground ham. Cover with 1 to 2 tablespoons Swiss cheese. Melt fat, add onion, and cook until soft. Make a cream sauce: Add seasonings to cream, blend flour with a little cream, then add rest of cream. Whip eggs and add cream sauce gradually beating well. Add in onion mixture, stir, and cook in top of double boiler over low heat until thickened. Stir constantly, preferably with a wooden spoon. Pour a little over the ham and cheese, filling pans not more than ⅔ full. Smooth surface, sprinkle with a little grated cheese, and bake in a hot oven, 450° F., until tartlets brown and filling is bubbly. Serve at once.

Swedish Meat Balls in Gravy (8 to 10 servings)

Sonya Hopkins, whose parents were born in Sweden, once appeared on my television program to show how a real Smörgåsbord is prepared. This prized recipe was one of the dishes, and one which Sonya's mother says won Sonya her husband. A certain male house guest tasted the meat balls, asked who had prepared them, and promptly proposed to the lady. Girls, take notice!

2 slices white bread with crusts
¼ cup milk
1 pound top beef, round or chuck (all fat removed), ground fine
1 small onion, peeled and grated
1 tablespoon minced parsley
1 egg
Salt and black pepper to taste
¼ teaspoon ground cloves
¼ teaspoon ground coriander seeds
¼ teaspoon ground allspice
4 tablespoons butter or margarine

Tear bread in pieces. Mix with milk to make a paste (mushy, but not runny). Do this with your hands. Combine with meat, onion, parsley, and egg. Mix in seasonings and spices. I used whole pieces, ground in my mortar, but use powdered ones if you prefer. If you can't buy coriander, leave it out. It adds a subtle flavor but is not absolutely necessary. Make a small meat ball, brown in a bit of butter, taste it to check seasonings. Correct if needed. Using about a teaspoonful, shape meat into balls and set aside.

Near party time, sauté meat balls in butter or margarine. Remove from pan. Prepare the following:

Gravy for Meat Balls

2 tablespoons flour
1¼ cups consommé or bouillon
Salt and pepper to taste
¼ teaspoon soy sauce
1 teaspoon Worcestershire sauce

Use the same pan. Add flour to butter or margarine in pan and stir until smooth. Have the heat low. Add liquid gradually, then seasonings. When thick and smooth, return meat balls and heat thoroughly.

To serve: Transfer Swedish Meat Balls and Gravy to a chafing dish or food warmer. Have a basket of tiny buttered buns (from the bakery), and let your guests make their own sandwiches.

Note: These meat balls freeze very well. They can also be made a day ahead and reheated for serving.

Chicken Livers in Bacon Jackets (About 30 hors d'oeuvre)

1 pound chicken livers (about 15)
¼ cup butter or margarine
Salt and pepper to taste
½ pound thinly-sliced breakfast bacon

Cut livers in half. Sauté in melted fat on both sides, stirring occasionally. Keep covered; livers pop badly. Cook 5 minutes over low heat, season, and let cool. Cut bacon slices in half with scissors. Wrap around livers, secure with a pick. This can be done the morning of the party. Refrigerate until ready to cook.

Brown livers in a skillet over low heat about 10 minutes, or in a 350° F. oven about 15 to 20 minutes. Drain on absorbent paper. To serve, put in a chafing dish set over boiling water. Keep covered.

New England Codfish or Haddock Balls (8 to 10 servings)

1 teaspoon melted butter
2 cups hot mashed potatoes
1 egg, well beaten
7-ounce can codfish or haddock flakes
½ teaspoon salt or more
¼ teaspoon black pepper
1 to 3 teaspoons flour

Add butter to the potatoes. Fold in the egg and fish, and season. Add just enough flour to make mixture hold together. Beat until well mixed. Refrigerate several hours or longer. Use a teaspoon of the mixture and shape into tiny balls, rolling between floured palms. Fry in a basket in deep fat 375° F. for 2 to 3 minutes or until golden brown. Then drain on absorbent paper. Serve in a chafing dish or food warmer over low heat. Have picks nearby for spearing.

Note: If salt cod is used, soak in water several hours or if very salty, overnight. Drain, cover with water, boil 20 minutes or until tender, and flake.

CHOICE PICKUPS

Curried Peanuts (8 servings)

Put 1 pound salted peanuts in a shallow pan. Heat in a 375° F. oven 15 to 20 minutes. Stir occasionally to keep from burning. Remove from oven. While still hot, stir in 3 or 4 tablespoons curry powder or more to taste. Cool, place in apothecary jars or on nut plates. These nuts keep very well in a tin box with a tight lid.

Deviled Pecans (4 or 5 servings)

Combine ½ pound pecans with 1½ teaspoons of Kitchen Spice (see recipe in Season to Taste section). Add 2 tablespoons olive oil and a tablespoon Worcestershire sauce. Mix well; use your fingers. Place in a shallow pan in a 375° F. oven for 15 to 20 minutes or until nuts brown. Stir occasionally. Cool, and add more spices and salt to taste.

Cheesy Popcorn (6 to 8 servings)

Melt ¼ cup butter in a deep skillet or Dutch oven. Stir in ½ to 1 teaspoon curry powder or more. Add 1 quart dry popped corn. Mix, then sprinkle 1 cup grated Cheddar cheese over. Stir until well distributed and corn is hot.

Note: Cheese may be omitted; the result is curried popcorn.

Sherried Olives (2 or 3 to a serving)

Drain jumbo ripe olives, soak overnight in sherry to cover. Drain and serve very cold.

Dilled Green Olives (2 or 3 to a serving)

Drain brine from an 8-ounce jar of jumbo green olives, not stuffed. Place in the jar:

1 garlic clove, split
1 slice hot red pepper or 1 tiny whole one
1 whole head of fresh dill or 1 teaspoon dried seeds
⅓ cup cider vinegar
⅔ cup salad oil or part olive oil
¼ teaspoon black pepper
Salt if needed, but add the next day

These olives keep indefinitely in the refrigerator. Keep cold until ready to serve.

Curried Potato Chips (6 to 8 servings)

In a 350° F. oven, heat ½ pound potato chips in a shallow pan until very hot. Remove from oven, sprinkle with 1 to 3 teaspoons curry powder. Mix with two forks to coat well. Cool and serve. (The potato chips may become soft when hot, but will be crisp again as soon as they cool.)

9 SOUP OF THE EVENING

Soup as the pièce de résistance of the meal is an ancient custom. Before the days of forks, it was difficult to eat daintily, with the fingers, a slab of meat hacked from a side of beef or a joint of mutton. Even the ewer of rose water and community towel, which were circulated around the table after the repast, were hardly sufficient to make the guests tidy. Hence, "hashes, soups, potages, ragouts, and the like," predominated at a banquet in the era when table implements were limited to spoons and knives.

By the eighteenth century, table traits had changed, and so had menus, influenced to a large degree by widespread use of the fork. This was the era of the groaning board. Soup from being the main dish became unimportant, merely one of many foods which made up the enormous collation called dinner.

Today we have relearned the advantages of making a meal of thick, nourishing soup. Remember the Mock Turtle's appraisal?

Beautiful soup, so rich and green,
Waiting in a hot tureen!
Who for such dainties would not stoop?
Soup of the evening, Beautiful Soup.

Do take the time the day before your party to make a fine full-bodied stock. You will find a 6-quart pressure cooker simplifies the preparation tremendously. If you have a handsome soup tureen, perhaps an old one with matching plates, by all means let soup be your modern pièce de résistance!

FIRST SERVED

Spiced Jellied Chicken Soup (8 servings)

This eighteenth-century recipe is from Mrs. Bradley's *British Housewife*. For summer cocktail-suppers, serve this soup garnished with slices of lemon. It is delicious hot, too.

5- to 6-pound fat hen
3 sprigs parsley
Small bunch celery leaves tied together
5 or 6 peppercorns or ¼ teaspoon ground pepper
1 tablespoon salt
½-inch-thick slice French bread, toasted
2 onions, peeled and sliced
3 whole cloves
1 bay leaf
¼ teaspoon each: summer savory, basil, thyme
1 blade mace or ⅛ teaspoon powdered mace
1 clove garlic, minced

If using a soup kettle, simmer all ingredients together in 3 quarts water, very slowly for 4 to 5 hours or until chicken is tender but not falling from the bones. Or cook in a pressure cooker (6-quart) for 50 minutes to an hour in 6 cups water at 15 pounds' pressure.

Sweetbread Vichyssoise (6 servings)

You can serve *this* vichyssoise (it tastes like chicken), when sweetbreads are on your menu, save quite a few pennies, yet not be repeating flavors.

3 large sweetbreads (1¼ to 1½ pounds)
1 quart water
1 heart celery or 4 small stalks with leaves
3 sprigs parsley
1 teaspoon salt (about)
⅛ teaspoon black pepper
1 onion, peeled

Put all ingredients in a Dutch oven or saucepan with a tight lid. Cover, let come to a boil, then simmer 45 minutes or until sweetbreads are fork tender. Cool sweetbreads in broth, remove them, and strain the stock. Prepare:

2 bunches shallots and tops, minced
1 small onion, peeled and sliced
1 medium potato, pared and sliced
Salt and pepper to taste
Dash cayenne or Tabasco
*¼ teaspoon Sensation Seasoner **
1 cup heavy cream
Paprika
Parsley or chives

Add everything but cream and garnish to sweetbread stock. Cover and simmer until vegetables are tender—30 to 40 minutes is usually enough. Strain. Put vegetables through a food mill or in a blender with a little liquid. Return to broth. Add cream and correct seasoning.

Serve chilled, dusted with paprika and a sprinkling of minced parsley or chives, or hot, garnished with croutons if desired.

MAIN-DISH SOUPS

Seacrest Fish Chowder (8 servings)

This is a specialty of Mrs. Mamie Newbolt's Seacrest Hotel, in Bimini. Meat is expensive in the Bahamas and has to be imported, but fish is plentiful, and most popular served in chowder.

½ cup butter, bacon drippings, or salt pork fat
4 onions, peeled and diced
2 stalks celery with leaves, diced
1 green pepper, diced (seeds removed)
4 potatoes, pared and sliced
3 carrots, scraped and cut in thin rings
1 garlic clove, minced
1 cup sliced okra or a 6-inch zucchini
3 cups canned or fresh tomatoes, peeled and diced
¼ teaspoon thyme
¼ teaspoon basil
⅛ teaspoon marjoram
¼ teaspoon soy sauce
¼ teaspoon M.S.G.
1 teaspoon sugar
2 teaspoons salt or more to taste
¼ teaspoon freshly-ground black pepper
½ teaspoon seasoning salt
1 slice hot red pepper or a tiny whole one
5 cups water
2½ to 3 pounds boned grouper or red snapper

Melt fat in bottom of soup kettle or Dutch oven. Add vegetables and cook until soft but not browned—about 10 minutes. Add seasonings and water. Let come to a hard boil. Cover, turn heat low and simmer ½ hour. Stir occasionally to prevent sticking. Add fish cut in serving pieces. Bring to a boil again, then lower heat, and cook 20 minutes, or until fish is done. Let stand a few hours before serving to bring out the flavors and mellow the chowder. Reheat and serve.

Note: It will take a 3- to 4-pound fish to yield this amount of boneless fish.

Dixie Sea-Food Gumbo, the Pressure-Cooker Way (10 to 12 servings)

This soup can be made a day ahead and reheated. To prepare the stock:

4- to 5-pound hen, cut in pieces
Flour (seasoned)
Chicken fat, lard, or shortening
½ cup water
2 onions, peeled and quartered
2 stalks celery with leaves
1 carrot, scraped
2 cloves garlic
Few sprigs parsley
1 bay leaf
¼ teaspoon thyme
1½ teaspoons salt
¼ teaspoon black pepper
Dash cayenne
1 teaspoon sugar
1 quart water

Roll chicken in flour. Melt fat in a 6-quart pressure cooker and fry chicken until golden. Pour off excess fat. Add ½ cup water and bring to a boil. Add all other ingredients, cover, and cook 50 minutes at 15 pounds' pressure. If chicken is not quite tender, cook under pressure another 10 to 15 minutes. Let cool in broth. Discard skin and bones; dice chicken. Strain and skim stock, then add chicken.

To make the Gumbo:

¼-pound-slice lean raw ham
2 tablespoons chicken fat or butter
1 quart okra, cut in thin rings
1 green pepper, minced
1 slice hot red pepper or dash of cayenne
1 pint fresh or frozen Lima beans
1 large onion, peeled and minced
1 quart canned tomatoes, or fresh, peeled and quartered
6 cups chicken stock

Sauté the ham in fat in bottom of pressure cooker (uncovered). Cut ham in small pieces. Add okra, peppers, Lima beans, and onion. Cook 5 to 10 minutes or until vegetables are soft. Stir occasionally; do not brown. Add tomatoes and stock. Cover cooker. Cook 5 minutes at 15 pounds' pressure.

(Or use a soup kettle and simmer ingredients about 40 minutes.) Remove from heat and set aside.

For the final touches, pour into a large kettle and add:

1 cup fresh or frozen corn, cut from cob
1 tablespoon filé powder
1 pound raw shrimp, peeled and cleaned
1 pound cooked crab meat
1 pint raw oysters
Salt and pepper (if needed)
Tabasco (if desired)

Bring soup to a slow boil. Add corn, filé powder (mixed to a paste with 2 tablespoons hot water), and shrimp. Cook about 15 minutes; then add crab meat and oysters. Simmer until oysters curl and are heated through (but *not* rubbery). Be careful not to let this very thick soup burn. Correct seasoning if necessary and serve.

To serve: Traditionally, gumbo is served in a deep tureen, a bowl of fluffy rice nearby. Each guest helps himself, first spooning a small amount of rice into his soup plate, then filling it with the gumbo.

Note: Some cooks prefer to leave the shrimp and crabs in their shells; the guests then pick the meat out themselves. This seems a rather messy procedure to me, but suit yourself.

Grand Central Station Oyster Bar Stew (6 servings)

Contrary to most opinions, this soup can be made ahead. In fact, it seems to mellow if allowed to stand for two hours or so at room temperature just after it is made. One word of warning—if the soup does stand, the oysters will shrink, but this won't affect the flavor. Here's my adaptation of what is perhaps America's favorite oyster stew.

2 cups heavy cream
2 cups milk
Salt and cayenne pepper
1 cup liquor from oysters or more, strained
1 cup canned clam juice (optional)
6 tablespoons butter
1 quart oysters, drained
1 teaspoon Worcestershire sauce
½ teaspoon paprika
½ teaspoon celery salt or seasoning salt
Extra butter (optional)

Scald cream and milk in a double boiler, covered. Add salt and cayenne to taste. Stir in liquor from oysters. (The original recipe calls for clam juice, but if you can't get it, leave it out—I seldom use it.) Cover. While this is heating, melt butter in a deep skillet. Add oysters and cook until edges curl; then add rest of seasonings. Pour liquids over oysters and heat until just below boiling, stirring constantly. Do not let boil. Pour into a tureen and serve in deep soup plates with oyster crackers. Put a pat of butter in each plate if you wish, but that's a little too rich for me.

War-Between-the-States Soup (12 servings)

This soup is appropriate for Thanksgiving because of its origin. The story goes that during the lean years of the Civil War, a family in Georgia had gathered to celebrate Thanksgiving Day. Each had contributed something, and finally a traditional meal was assembled. As they sat down, there was a knock at the door—a group of hungry Confederate soldiers were asking for something to eat. Whereupon the hostess had an inspiration. She sent all suitable food to the kitchen to be simmered with some broth into a thick potage. It was so delicious that the recipe was written down and christened War-Between-the-States Soup.

Don't be discouraged by the number of ingredients. It is easy to make this soup, and it can be prepared well ahead. Remember it is a *main* dish; only bread and dessert are needed to round out a grand meal.

4- to 5-pound chicken or turkey
1 large bunch celery tops
4 sprigs parsley
1 tiny red pepper or dash cayenne
1 clove garlic
¼ teaspoon M.S.G. (optional)
Salt, pepper or peppercorns
Consommé (if needed)
1 cup celery, diced
1 cup small pickling onions or peeled, minced shallots
1 teaspoon celery salt
1 teaspoon garlic salt
10-ounce package frozen succotash
10-ounce package frozen peas and carrots
1 cup cooked rice
½ pound fresh mushrooms
2 tablespoons melted fat
2 or 3 tablespoons flour
1 cup heavy cream or evaporated milk (about)
1½ teaspoons soy sauce
1 cup minced cooked ham
1 canned pimiento, minced

Place chicken or turkey in a 6-quart pressure cooker. Add 6 cups water, celery tops, parsley, red pepper or cayenne, garlic, M.S.G., 1 tablespoon salt, and ¼ teaspoon pepper or peppercorns. Cover. Steam for 60 minutes at 15 pounds' pressure. If meat is not tender, cook 10 to 15 minutes longer. (Or simmer in a soup kettle with 2 to 3 quarts water, 3 to 4 hours, or until tender.) Cool fowl in broth. Remove fat and strain broth. If needed, add consommé or water to make about 7 cups. Discard skin and bones; dice chicken or turkey meat.

Return broth to pressure cooker. Add celery, onions or shallots, celery and garlic salt. Cover and cook 5 minutes at 15 pounds' pressure (or 20 minutes in a soup kettle). Then mix in frozen vegetables and rice. Simmer until tender.

Rinse mushrooms, sliver, and sauté 3 minutes in melted fat. Add 2 tablespoons flour mixed with cream or evaporated milk, stir till thick. Add soy sauce. Pour into soup. Stir in ham, pimiento, and diced chicken or turkey. Add salt and pepper if needed. Reheat and stir. If soup is not the consistency of thick cream, add another tablespoon of flour mixed to a paste with a little cream; simmer a few minutes longer. Then serve, or let stand and reheat at party time.

Regency Dandy's Oxtail Soup (8 to 10 servings)

When King George IV was England's Regent, and Beau Brummell the arbiter of fashion, Oxtail Soup was a great favorite of bucks and dandies. Here's a streamlined pressure-cooker version of this hearty, full-bodied dish.

4 tablespoons butter, margarine, or olive oil
2 oxtails cut in 2- to 3-inch pieces (about 3 pounds)
2 tablespoons flour
1 bunch celery and leaves, diced
4 large onions, peeled and diced
4 carrots, scraped and cut in rings
3 small turnips, peeled and shredded
2 cloves garlic, mashed
2 large marrow bones with or without meat
1 cup tomato catsup
2 tablespoons Worcestershire sauce
*1 teaspoon Browning * or Kitchen Bouquet*
½ teaspoon soy sauce
2 bay leaves
¼ teaspoon each: dried basil, thyme, marjoram or rosemary
4 whole cloves
4 whole allspice berries
¼ teaspoon M.S.G.
¼ teaspoon black pepper
Dash cayenne (optional)
1½ tablespoons salt
1 teaspoon sugar
6 cups water
½ cup port, sherry, or Madeira
¼ cup chopped parsley

Melt fat in bottom of a 6-quart pressure cooker. Add oxtails sprinkled with flour. Cook until well browned; then remove and set aside. In the same fat, sauté the vegetables 5 to 10 minutes—until soft, not browned. Return oxtails, add other ingredients, except wine and parsley. Cook 50 minutes at 15 pounds' pressure or until oxtails are done. Open cooker, remove large marrow bones, let cool, and skim fat. (If soup is refrigerated, fat rises to top in a solid cake and is easily removed.) Just before serving, reheat. Take from stove, stir in wine. Garnish with parsley.

Or simmer 4 to 5 hours in a covered kettle, stir often, and watch to see mixture does not stick. This is fine to freeze.

Philadelphia Pepper Pot (12 servings)

In Colonial Philadelphia, "Free Women of Color" used to ring a bell through the streets, crying: "Good and hot, pepper pot." An iron kettle on a brazier in a wheelbarrow-like contraption held the savory soup. Housewives rushed to the door, tureen and reticule in hand, to buy the delicious soup for dinner. This recipe probably originated in the West Indies, where today "pepper pot" is a year-round favorite, the kettle kept constantly simmering on the stove, replenished from time to time, but never allowed to become exhausted.

1 pound honeycomb tripe
2 calf's feet or 1 veal knuckle with meat
3 quarts water
2 onions, peeled and chopped
1 tablespoon chives, minced
2 leeks or 6 shallots, chopped
1 clove garlic, minced
1 bunch celery tops
2 sprigs parsley, chopped
¼ teaspoon each: dried thyme, marjoram
1 bay leaf
2 whole cloves
1 blade mace
¼ to ½ teaspoon white or black peppercorns
1 small hot red pepper
1 tablespoon salt
2 medium potatoes, pared and diced
2 carrots, scraped and cut in rings
1 medium turnip, pared and diced
½ cup chopped celery
Soup Dumplings (as below)
½ cup cream
½ cup white wine

Wipe meat carefully, place in soup kettle with water, onions, chives, leeks or shallots, garlic, celery tops, herbs, spices, and seasonings. Cover, simmer 2 to 3 hours, or until tripe is very tender. Strain broth and skim. Cut tripe into shreds. Cube veal and discard bones. Return meat and broth to kettle and add vegetables. Cook 1 hour or until vegetables are done.

Soup Dumplings

½ cup sifted flour
⅛ teaspoon salt
1 teaspoon baking powder
2 tablespoons shortening
1 tablespoon minced parsley (optional)
2 to 3 tablespoons milk

Sift dry ingredients together. Add shortening and blend with fingers until mixture resembles coarse bread crumbs. Add parsley, if you are using it, and just enough milk to make a stiff dough. Roll ¼-inch thick on a floured board. Cut out dumplings with a tiny vegetable cutter, a floured thimble, or top of a catsup bottle. Or cut dough in ½-inch squares with a dull knife or pastry wheel.

Stir cream into soup. Place dumplings side by side on top of soup, cover, and simmer 10 to 15 minutes. Do not remove lid until 10 minutes are up. If dumplings are not done, steam a few minutes longer. They should be light.

Make the pepper pot and dumplings a day ahead if you wish. Just before serving, heat and add wine.

Pressure-cooker method: Steam tripe and ingredients listed for first cooking in a 6-quart cooker with *6 cups water,* at 15 pounds' pressure for 1 hour. Open cooker, strain and skim broth. Cut up meat and return with broth to cooker. Add vegetables; cook 5 minutes at 15 pounds' pressure. Prepare dumplings and proceed as above.

Vegetable Potpourri (8 to 10 servings)

The vegetables in this soup vary according to season, but the stock remains the same. Make the stock a day or two before adding the vegetables.

Basic Meat Stock:

1½ pounds oxtails or 1 pound lean beef chuck, cut in pieces
2 large marrow bones with meat
1 tablespoon fat, if needed
2 carrots, scraped and sliced
2 large onions, peeled and sliced
1 bunch celery tops tied together
3 sprigs parsley
2 cloves garlic, sliced
1 bay leaf
¼ teaspoon each: thyme, basil or rosemary, black pepper
2 whole cloves
2 whole allspice berries
¼ teaspoon soy sauce
Dash cayenne or Tabasco
¼ teaspoon M.S.G.
1 tablespoon salt

Brown oxtails or chuck and marrow bones in bottom of 6-quart pressure cooker, using fat if necessary. When meat is browned, add all other ingredients and 6 cups water. Cover and cook 50 minutes at 15 pounds' pressure. (Or use a soup kettle: Add 3 quarts water, cover, and simmer all 2½ to 3 hours.) Cool and strain. Refrigerate, then remove cake of fat. Return meat, chopped from marrow bones, and oxtails (as they are), or chuck to broth.

Midsummer Variety

6 cups meat stock
2½ cups peeled quartered tomatoes
4 small zucchini, cut in ¼-inch slices
½ small head green cabbage, shredded
1 cup green beans, diced
½ pound okra, cut in thin rings
2 carrots, scraped and sliced
1 cup Lima beans
1 green pepper, diced
Corn cut from 6 ears
1 medium onion, peeled and minced
1 bunch shallots and tops, diced
2 stalks celery and leaves, minced
6-ounce can tomato purée, diluted with 1 can water (optional)
1 teaspoon sugar
½ teaspoon M.S.G.
Salt
Black pepper

Place all ingredients in 6-quart pressure cooker. Cover and cook 5 minutes at 15 pounds' pressure. If any vegetables are not tender, cook a minute or two longer, but avoid overcooking. Or simmer vegetables 1 hour in covered soup kettle or Dutch oven. Correct seasoning if necessary.

Note: If soup needs more body, add a little Worcestershire sauce, Kitchen Bouquet or Browning.* A beef bouillon cube or a little B.V. paste also helps.

Thick Vegetable Soup:

Add 1 cup cooked barley or rice, or more if desired, for a heartier potage.

Springtime Vegetable Soup:

Substitute 2 cups fresh green peas for zucchini and Lima beans. Or make whatever changes you like.

10 IF IT SWIMS

If you live near the sea, where you can buy a variety of fresh fish, you will often be tempted to serve it for cocktail-suppers. During the summer, Kennebec salmon is usually available, and it makes one of the finest of all main dishes. Serve it hot with an unusual fish butter or sauce, or cold, coated with jellied fish broth, or in an interesting variation of mayonnaise. Lake trout, red snapper, or whitefish are fine, too. Frozen or canned fish offer year-round possibilities.

You can poach or bake fish, use it whole, sliced or flaked, serve it hot or cold. When your cocktail-supper involves a number of guests, you may find it easier to serve fish flaked. It can be stretched by the addition of hard-cooked eggs, sautéed mushrooms, or varied with fresh or canned shellfish. Use one of the combinations suggested in this chapter, or vary to suit your needs. Keep hot until serving time in a chafing dish or food warmer.

All these recipes lend themselves to ahead-of-party preparation. And you'll find heatproof platters or enameled baking dishes fine for cooking and serving them.

FISH OVER THE COUNTER

Kennebec Salmon Ring with Lobster Sauce (6 servings)

This is a really elegant dish and one which will be greatly admired. For best results, use fresh lobster and salmon but frozen or canned may be substituted. Poach the salmon as directed on page 100, then flake.

2 cups cooked flaked salmon
2 eggs, separated
1/4 teaspoon paprika
1/8 teaspoon black pepper
Salt
1 small onion, peeled and grated
2 teaspoons Worcestershire sauce
Dash Tabasco or cayenne
1 cup whipped cream or rich cream sauce
Parsley

Add to the salmon all other ingredients, folding in stiffly-beaten egg whites and whipped cream or cream sauce last. Taste for seasoning, add more if needed. Spoon mixture into a well-greased ring mold. Set mold in a pan a quarter full of warm water. Place in a 375° F. oven. Cook until mixture is firm but not dry, about 25 to 30 minutes. Remove salmon ring from mold with a dull knife, turn out on a round platter. Garnish with parsley sprigs and fill center with:

Lobster Sauce:

1 cup cooked lobster, cut in 1-inch chunks
3 tablespoons butter
1 1/2 tablespoons flour
1/2 cup milk
1/2 cup cream
Salt and pepper
1/8 teaspoon paprika
Dash Tabasco or cayenne
Lobster tomalley, mashed (optional)
Lobster coral, diced (optional)

Sauté lobster chunks in melted butter. Mix flour to a paste with milk. Add the cream. Pour onto lobster meat, stirring until sauce thickens. Remove from heat. Add other ingredients, blending well. Cover and let stand 2 hours before reheating and serving. Standing *improves* the flavor considerably.

Variation: Substitute 1 cup cooked shrimp for the lobster.

Cream of Curry Sauce (8 servings)

This sauce is delicious on any cooked flaked fish or shellfish, or a combination of both, enough for 2 pounds.

½ cup butter, margarine, drippings or chicken fat
¼ cup minced onion
⅓ cup flour
5 or 6 teaspoons curry powder or more
Salt
2 tablespoons Worcestershire sauce
1 teaspoon Kitchen Bouquet or Browning *
2 cups milk
1 cup cream or evaporated milk

Melt fat in a large saucepan or Dutch oven. Brown onion lightly, stirring constantly. Add flour and cook until very dark brown. Watch that it does not burn. Mix in curry powder and salt, and slowly pour on liquids, which have been beaten together. Never stop stirring. When thick and smooth, add fish. This can be made ahead and reheated.

Poached Lake Trout (8 servings)

Once when we were in Italy visiting friends in Turin, we were served a delectable poached trout—caught that very afternoon. The skin had been scraped off and the fish showered lightly with parsley. It was flanked by small tureens of melted butter with a faint suggestion of sweet Italian lemons, and a thin hollandaise. After much coaxing the cook gave me the recipe which was translated by our host. Try this with Lemon Sauce (below) instead of hollandaise, as Lemon Sauce has the special merit of standing without separating. And any fish, red snapper, salmon, pike, bass or whatever you prefer, is good this way.

To Poach Whole Fish

2 two-pound or a four-pound lake trout, red snapper, etc.
1 small onion, peeled and sliced
1 carrot, scraped and sliced
2 stalks celery with leaves, diced
3 sprigs parsley
Few sprigs thyme or ¼ teaspoon dried
¼ cup wine vinegar
½ cup white wine
1 teaspoon salt (about)
¼ teaspoon black pepper
6 cups water

Tie fish loosely, but securely, in cheesecloth. Add other ingredients to water and simmer 5 minutes. Then immerse fish and cook gently, allowing 10 to 12 minutes per pound. Lift out and drain, remove cheesecloth, and scrape off skin. Sprinkle with the chopped parsley just before serving. And serve the Lemon Sauce on the side.

Lemon Sauce (8 servings)

4 tablespoons butter
2 tablespoons flour
2 cups fish stock, chicken broth, or water
Juice of ½ lemon
Salt and pepper
Dash Tabasco
2 egg yolks, slightly beaten
4 tablespoons chopped parsley

Melt butter in top of double boiler. Add flour and stir to make a paste. Add broth slowly, stirring constantly, then add lemon juice and seasonings. Cook until the consistency of thin white sauce. Remove from heat, cool a little. Then beat in the egg yolks. Sprinkle with parsley and serve. If you have a blender, put everything into it at once and whip until smooth; *then* put in top of double boiler, stir constantly, and cook until thick.

Note: Substitute 1 whole egg for the 2 yolks if using blender, otherwise not.

Hard-cooked Egg Sauce:
Prepare Lemon Sauce as above, but for egg yolks substitute, just before serving, 2 chopped hard-cooked eggs. Sprinkle with a tablespoon of minced chives.

Olive-and-Parsley Sauce:
Prepare Lemon Sauce and add ½ cup sliced, stuffed olives.

Chilled Columbia River Salmon Steaks (8 servings)

Poach 8 salmon steaks (about ½ pound each) in the same ingredients given above for the whole fish. Do not wrap them. Allow 10 to 15 minutes for cooking depending on the thickness of steaks. Chill steaks well before removing skin. Serve with Caper Mayonnaise (see recipe).

Baked Creole Red Snapper (6 servings)

3-pound red snapper (weighed after head and tail removed)
1 clove garlic, crushed
1 teaspoon salt (about)
¼ teaspoon black pepper
5 tablespoons melted fat (olive oil, bacon fat, butter, or margarine)
1 tablespoon lemon juice
4 stalks celery, chopped
½ green pepper
2 onions, peeled and chopped
½ teaspoon sugar
2 cups canned or fresh tomatoes, peeled
2 tablespoons chopped parsley
¼ teaspoon thyme
1 bay leaf
Dash soy sauce
Worcestershire sauce to taste
Flour
Parsley for garnish

Clean snapper. Rub inside and out with a mixture of garlic, salt, pepper, fat, and lemon juice. Let stand in a cool place 1 hour. Place snapper in roasting pan. Add all other ingredients except flour and put in a 375° F. oven. Cook 1 hour, or until fish is done—split and see. Remove carefully to a serving dish. Or use a pretty enameled baking dish which can come right to the buffet table.

If necessary, thicken gravy with a flour-and-water paste: 1 tablespoon flour beaten with 3 tablespoons water for every cup gravy. Sprinkle snapper with chopped parsley.

Whitefish Madeira (8 servings)

3 to 4 cups cooked flaked whitefish
¼ cup butter or margarine
¼ cup flour
Salt, pepper, paprika to taste
½ teaspoon sugar
1 tablespoon Worcestershire sauce
Dash Tabasco
1 cup cream
1 cup milk
2 well-beaten egg yolks
¼ cup Madeira

For the fish, prepare this Madeira sauce. Melt butter or margarine in top of a double boiler. Add flour and seasonings. Stir to a smooth paste, gradually add cream and milk. Stir until very, very thick. (All this can be done ahead.) When ready to serve, add fish and heat thoroughly. Then remove from stove, stir in egg yolks. Add wine at the last minute. (A blender simplifies the mixing since all ingredients except the fish and wine can be put in at one time, whipped until smooth, and poured into the double boiler to be stirred until thick.) Spoon into patty shells or serve on rice.

Note: You can also prepare fillet of flounder, fillet of sole, halibut, pike, bass this way.

Variation: Add 1 cup of cooked shrimp or diced cooked lobster to the whitefish, or substitute for part of it. Oysters, sautéed in a little butter until plump but not hard, are also a good addition.

Cold Red Snapper with Jellied Lemon-Egg Sauce (6 servings)

This recipe from Natchez, Mississippi, is a summertime, Friday-night specialty there. It makes a delightfully different cocktail-supper main dish and one which can, and should be prepared 24 hours ahead.

- *3-pound red snapper (after head and tail removed)*
- *1 clove garlic*
- *Salt and cayenne*
- *¼ teaspoon ginger or 1-inch piece fresh ginger root*
- *½ lemon, juice and rind (about)*
- *½ cup olive oil*
- *1 onion, peeled and sliced in rings*
- *2 shallots and tops, minced*
- *1½ tablespoons flour*
- *3 to 4 cups hot water*
- *1 egg, well beaten*
- *3 tablespoons minced parsley and more for garnish*

Clean fish, wash well, remove all scales. Rub with crushed garlic, salt, cayenne, ginger, and lemon. Cover. Let stand at least 2 hours in refrigerator.

Heat oil in a flameproof enameled pan, cook onion, shallots and tops until soft, stirring occasionally. Add flour and brown, then slowly add water, stirring to make a thin sauce. When liquid boils, place snapper in pan, cover, and simmer about 30 minutes or until fish is done. If water cooks too low, add a little more. (Or cut snapper into 1-inch-thick slices and simmer 15 minutes.)

Strain broth. Measure 2 cups and bring to a boil. While still hot pour slowly over the egg, beating constantly (use an electric beater if possible). Taste for seasoning, add extra lemon juice if necessary. Stir in parsley. Chill snapper and sauce *separately*. When sauce stiffens a little (it should be like mayonnaise) spoon over fish, scraping off the skin first, if you prefer. Re-chill, garnish with extra parsley, and serve.

Sea Bass in Herbed Mushroom-Tomato Sauce (8 servings)

4- to 5-pound sea bass or 2 smaller ones
2 large onions, peeled and chopped
1 green pepper, chopped
6 stalks celery, chopped
1 garlic clove, mashed
3 tablespoons olive oil, bacon, or chicken fat
3 tablespoons butter or margarine
Salt and red pepper
1 quart tomatoes, fresh or canned
¼ teaspoon thyme
¼ teaspoon basil
1 bay leaf
1 teaspoon sugar (if tomatoes are acid)
½ pound fresh mushrooms, caps and stems separated
2 tablespoons butter

Poach and flake the sea bass. (Directions are on page 100.) There should be 3 to 4 cups. Prepare the sauce. Sauté onions, green pepper, celery, and garlic in fat until soft but not browned—about 5 minutes. Add all other ingredients, except mushrooms, 2 tablespoons of the butter, and the sea bass. Cover and simmer 25 to 30 minutes. The mixture should become thick and pasty. Add mushrooms sautéed in the remaining butter in a covered skillet for 5 minutes. Let all cook to blend. Combine with bass, heat thoroughly. Correct seasoning. Pour into a plain rice ring or over a mound of fluffy rice.

Note: Add 1 to 2 tablespoons curry to the above recipe when sautéing the vegetables or use ½ teaspoon powdered Spanish saffron. Either gives an intriguing flavor. You can also use salmon or haddock for an excellent dish.

Baked Halibut in Pickled Walnut Sauce (8 servings)

This sauce is popular in England where we enjoyed it for the first time on turbot at lovely Windermere in the Lake District. It is delicious with any bland fish, and I have substituted halibut for turbot with success.

Select 2 thick slices, about 2 pounds each, wipe, spread with ½ cup butter, and place in a shallow baking dish. (Use 2 dishes if necessary.) Sprinkle with pepper but no salt. Bake in a 375° F. oven about 30 minutes.

Prepare 2 cups medium white sauce, omitting salt. Stir in 12 crushed pickled walnuts (drained first). Cover and let stand. About 5 minutes before fish is done, spoon sauce over slices, bake 10 minutes longer, and serve. Garnish with parsley sprigs.

Spanish Orange Sole (8 servings)

¼ cup olive oil
12 small shallots and tops, minced
½ pound fresh mushrooms, slivered
8 large fillets of sole
Salt and pepper
1 cup white wine
½ cup orange juice
¼ teaspoon M.S.G.
¼ teaspoon soy sauce
½ teaspoon salt or more
⅓ cup curaçao or Triple Sec
¼ cup butter
Chopped parsley
Paprika

Use a shallow, copper baking dish or a pretty pottery one. Pour in the olive oil. Add half the shallots and half the mushrooms. Place the fillets side by side in the dish. Season lightly with salt and black pepper. Pour on wine, then orange juice, and add seasonings and liqueur. Sprinkle the rest of the shallots and mushrooms over and dot with butter. Bake in a 350° F. oven, 40 minutes or until sole is done and beginning to brown on top. Baste occasionally during baking. Garnish with parsley and paprika. If placed on a warming plate, the fillets will keep hot without drying out during the serving period.

Baked Fillet of Sole with Capers (8 servings)

¾ cup butter or part margarine
Salt and pepper
8 serving pieces fillet of sole or flounder
Flour
2 tablespoons capers
2 tablespoons caper or wine vinegar
1 teaspoon anchovy paste
Chopped parsley
Paprika

Spread ¼ cup butter over the bottom of a large, flat copper or pottery baking dish, one you can bring to the table. Salt and pepper the fillets lightly. Roll them in flour, shaking off any excess. Place fillets side by side in the baking dish. Dot with rest of the butter. Bake in a 350° F. oven, basting occasionally, 30 to 35 minutes or until fillets seem tender and begin to brown. Add the capers. Mix vinegar with anchovy paste, and pour over the fish; baste well. Bake 5 to 10 minutes longer. When liquid is bubbling again, remove from oven, sprinkle parsley and paprika over fish, and take to the table. Place the baking dish over a candle warmer or hot plate to keep fish hot during serving period.

Note: Fillet of channel catfish is equally delicious prepared by the same recipe.

Herbed Fillet of Flounder (8 servings)

Follow the above recipe for preparing and baking the fillets. In place of capers, vinegar, and anchovies, use: 2 tablespoons lemon juice or white wine vinegar, 1 tablespoon fresh minced tarragon, thymc, basil, or any preferred herb, (or ½ teaspoon dried herb) and a dash of Tabasco. Garnish with chopped parsley and sprinkle paprika on the fillets.

SHELL-OUTS

Shellfish is a boon to the hostess; it can always be prepared beforehand and added to sauces at the last minute. Shellfish keeps its flavor well in a chafing dish or food warmer. Here follow some tried-and-true recipes, each a little out of the ordinary, any of which will delight sea-food fans.

Baltimore Crab Cakes (about 10 cakes)

3 tablespoons butter
1 small onion, peeled and grated
3 tablespoons flour
½ cup milk
½ cup cream
⅛ teaspoon nutmeg
Dash M.S.G.
¼ teaspoon dry mustard
2 teaspoons Worcestershire sauce
Dash each: Tabasco, soy sauce
½ teaspoon salt or more to taste
1 egg
2 tablespoons minced parsley
1 pound cooked crab meat, back fin preferred
Bread crumbs, freshly made
¼ cup butter or margarine

Melt 3 tablespoons butter in a skillet. Add onion and brown slightly. Add flour, mix to a smooth paste. Gradually pour in milk and cream, stirring constantly as sauce thickens. Add all seasonings. Stir in lightly-beaten egg. Mix well and cook until sauce is very thick. Remove from heat and cool. Then add parsley and, using two forks, fold in crab meat. Try not to break up large pieces. Put in a bowl, cover, and chill in refrigerator—preferably overnight.

To make cakes: Take a heaping tablespoon of the crab mixture, roll into a ball between floured palms, dip in bread crumbs. (Each cake should be about 3 inches across and ½ inch thick.) Melt the ¼ cup butter or margarine in a skillet. Brown cakes on both sides, then serve. I have fried these cakes ahead and reheated them in a hot skillet without any fat. Or you can reheat them in a hot (450° F.) oven.

Dixie Deviled Crabs (6 servings)

Here's another recipe cherished in the deep South. The deviled crab is usually served in large crab shells, but if you can't get them, use scallop shells or individual shallow baking dishes.

2/3 cup consommé or milk
3 slices white bread
1 egg
2 tablespoons butter or margarine
1 small onion, peeled and minced
1 clove garlic, mashed
1 pound fresh cooked crab meat, back fin preferred
Salt, pepper, cayenne to taste
2 tablespoons chopped parsley
1 tablespoon Worcestershire sauce
2 or 3 tablespoons sherry
1/4 cup bread or cracker crumbs
1/2 cup grated Parmesan or Swiss cheese
6 teaspoons butter

Mix consommé or milk with bread to a mush. Add egg and combine well. Melt the 2 tablespoons butter or margarine in a skillet; lightly brown onion and garlic. Add bread mixture to skillet and cook until it all holds together. Do not let mixture get too stiff. Stir constantly. Remove from heat, fold into crab meat, seasonings, parsley, Worcestershire, and sherry. Pile into crab shells or shallow dishes. This can be prepared the day before using. Cover and refrigerate.

To serve, mix crumbs with grated cheese and sprinkle freely over deviled crab. Dot each shell with a teaspoon of butter. Place side by side on a cooky sheet in a 400° F. oven for 10 minutes or until heated through. Then put under broiler until cheese and crumbs form a browned crunchy topping. These shells will remain hot on a warming tray.

Variation: If you are partial to the flavor of herbs, omit sherry, add 1/4 teaspoon thyme and marjoram or rosemary, 1/8 teaspoon each nutmeg and ginger. Or 1/4 teaspoon saffron is very good in place of ginger and nutmeg.

Pickwick Café Crab Meat Gratin (6 servings)

The Pickwick Café in Montgomery, Alabama, was famous for its sea food—especially this recipe.

Divide 1 pound cooked crab meat (lump meat or back fin) among 6 shallow individual baking dishes. Cover with ¼ cup of the rich Cheese Sauce which follows. (This can be prepared beforehand.) When ready to cook, sprinkle each baking dish with a teaspoon of bread crumbs, a teaspoon of butter, and add a tablespoon of heavy cream. Last of all, sprinkle over a tablespoon of grated aged Cheddar cheese. Heat 10 minutes in a 400° F. oven, then run dishes under broiler until top browns and cheese is bubbly. Serve at once or place on warming tray.

Cheese Sauce:

3 tablespoons butter
3 tablespoons flour
1¼ cups milk
¼ cup cream
¼ pound aged Cheddar cheese, cubed
2 egg yolks
1 whole egg
¼ teaspoon salt or more to taste
3 drops Tabasco or dash cayenne
¼ teaspoon paprika
1 teaspoon Worcestershire sauce

Put ingredients in a blender and whip until smooth. Transfer to top of a double boiler, cook until cheese melts and sauce is thick, stirring constantly. Or make sauce in top of double boiler; melt butter, add flour, make a smooth paste, then add milk, cream, and cheese. Stir until cheese melts, then add well-beaten yolks and egg, and seasonings. Cook until smooth and thick.

Baltimore Crab Imperial (8 servings)

2 pounds fresh cooked crab meat, back fin preferred
1 green pepper, minced
1 canned pimiento, minced
1 small onion, peeled and grated
2 tablespoons minced celery
2 teaspoons dry mustard
2 teaspoons minced capers or more
Salt
Tabasco
1 teaspoon Worcestershire sauce
2 eggs, well beaten
⅔ to 1 cup mayonnaise

This superb creation can be served hot or cold. If cold, put crab meat into a bowl, flake gently with a fork. Try not to separate the lumps, but remove all shell. Add other ingredients, taste for seasoning, and add more as needed. Combine with mayonnaise last of all; add just enough to bind ingredients. In Baltimore, a mound of crab meat (made with an ice cream scoop or coffee cup) is placed on cleaned crab shells. Frost salad lightly with extra mayonnaise if you wish, and garnish with extra bits of green pepper, capers, and pimiento. A slice of hard-cooked egg gives added color.

To serve hot, put crab meat in shells or ramekins, heat in a 350° F. oven about 15 to 20 minutes. When heated through, bring to the table. It will remain warm on a heating unit.

Wednesday's Oysters (8 servings)

In the days when I had cooks—and cooks had nights out —I used to concoct my quick Wednesday's Oysters. It is filling served over rice, noodles, in patty shells, or on toast points, and is still known as a specialty of the house.

1 pound fresh mushrooms
1 cup minced celery
1 large onion, peeled and minced
Salt and black pepper
½ cup butter
1 quart oysters
¼ teaspoon soy sauce
¼ teaspoon M.S.G.
1½ to 2 tablespoons cornstarch
¾ cup cream or evaporated milk
½ cup minced parsley

Wash and sliver mushrooms, mix with celery, onion, salt, and pepper. Sauté in butter 3 or 4 minutes in a large skillet or Dutch oven until soft but not browned. Add drained oysters, cook about 5 minutes or until plump and thoroughly heated, but not hard. Stir occasionally. Add soy sauce, M.S.G., and cornstarch mixed to a paste with cream or milk and a little of the oyster liquor if you wish. Keep stirring and when mixture has thickened, add parsley, correct seasonings and serve. (If oysters are unusually watery you may have to add more cornstarch and cream.) For guests fond of oysters, this is your dish.

Note: Prepare ahead of time if you want; the oysters will shrink but they are still delicious.

Variation: Add 1 diced, canned pimiento, 1 tablespoon Worcestershire sauce, 1 teaspoon Browning * or Kitchen Bouquet, and ½ cup sherry or Madeira to oysters just before serving. Stretch recipe with 4 sliced hard-cooked eggs.

Lobster Tails in Bourbon Sauce (6 servings)

For a festive touch, make the Bourbon Sauce in a chafing dish right at your buffet table.

4 large lobster tails, fresh or frozen, weighing ¾ to 1 pound each
Salt and black pepper
½ cup melted butter

Have lobster tails split down *top side,* not underside. Salt and pepper well, and brush with butter. Grill 5 minutes on each side, continuing to baste with butter. If lobster meat is not done, cook a little longer. Remove from broiler, let cool enough to handle. Strain off butter to use later. Take lobster from shells and dice it into 1-inch pieces. Set aside. This can be prepared several hours beforehand.

Bourbon Sauce:

Butter from lobsters
2-ounce can truffles or 6-ounce can sliced mushrooms
Salt and pepper
¼ teaspoon paprika
¼ teaspoon Tabasco
1 teaspoon Worcestershire sauce
½ teaspoon soy sauce
Lobster meat
6 egg yolks
1 pint heavy cream or light cream mixed with 1 tablespoon flour
¼ cup bourbon whisky or more
½ teaspoon sugar, if needed

Melt butter in chafing dish set over water or in top of double boiler. Add slivered truffles or mushrooms (drained) and seasonings. Mix in lobster and heat through. Fold in egg yolks well beaten with cream. Stir over low heat until mixture is hot; do not allow to boil. Add whisky and taste, adding sugar only if needed. Serve at once.

Note: Cooked shrimp, scallops, or any other sea food can be substituted for lobster.

Coquilles Saint-Jacques (8 servings)
(Scallops Baked in Shells)

1 cup white wine
2 pounds scallops (bay scallops preferred)
2 stalks celery, diced
3 sprigs parsley
Salt and pepper
¼ teaspoon M.S.G.
¼ teaspoon soy sauce
2 tablespoons minced shallots or onions (peeled)
1 pound mushrooms, slivered
½ cup butter or margarine
2 tablespoons flour
4 egg yolks
1 cup heavy cream
¼ cup chopped parsley
8 tablespoons butter
½ cup bread crumbs

Bring wine to a boil, then add scallops, celery, parsley sprigs, and seasonings. Cover and simmer 5 minutes or until scallops are done. Strain broth and set aside. If scallops are large, cut in half. Sauté shallots or onions and mushrooms in melted butter or margarine until soft but not browned. Mix in flour to a smooth paste, then gradually stir in broth. Add egg yolks beaten with cream. Turn heat low; stir until sauce is well blended and thickened. Fold in scallops, heat, add parsley and spoon into scallop shells or individual shallow baking dishes. Brown crumbs in 8 tablespoons butter and sprinkle over scallops. This can be prepared the morning of the party.

To serve: Place in a 400° F. oven and heat 8 to 10 minutes. Do not overcook. Brown under broiler if necessary. Serve at once.

Variation: Pipe mashed potatoes around each dish before final heating in oven. Brown under broiler and serve.

Shrimp, Ann Jeffries (12 servings)

Ann Jeffries, who was a superb cook, gave me this recipe after I raved about it at her home. It is a delicious dish and at its best when served over a tall mound of fluffy rice. Make the sauce a day ahead.

½ cup butter
¾ cup drippings, chicken fat, or olive oil
3 onions, peeled and minced
3 large cloves garlic, minced
2 (10-ounce) packages frozen okra, or 1 quart fresh
Salt and pepper
1 tablespoon filé powder
¾ teaspoon M.S.G.
1 teaspoon thyme (or half thyme, half orégano)
¾ cup chopped parsley
2 No. 2½ cans tomatoes
1 tablespoon sugar if needed
5 pounds shrimp, boiled, peeled, and de-veined
1 pound fresh cooked crab meat

Heat butter and other fat in bottom of large Dutch oven or kettle with a tight lid. Add onions and garlic and cook about 5 minutes, until lightly browned. Add okra, seasonings, herbs, tomatoes, and sugar if tomatoes are acid. Cover, bring to boiling, then turn heat as low as possible and simmer slowly, 4 to 6 hours. Stir frequently to keep from sticking and scorching. Mixture should be a thick sauce, but not dry.

At serving time: Heat sauce, add shrimp, and as soon as it is hot, pour into a tureen. Sprinkle with crab meat.

Note: Ann used a tablespoon of thyme and orégano mixed; you can add that much if you like a stronger herb flavor.

Shellfish in Sauces:

Any shellfish—shrimp, oysters, lobster, or what you will—can be mixed with any of the sauces given in this chapter. Use an equal amount of cooked shellfish for the amount of boiled or flaked fish required.

11 UNDER COVER

Casserole cookery is older than Methuselah. Very likely the Egyptians used covered earthen dishes for baking even before the departure of the Children of Israel. Today the French are famous for their under-cover cookery. Indeed, casserole dishes are popular everywhere.

A friend of mine uses them to special advantage. She doubles casserole recipes, and bakes in two foil-lined casseroles for freezing. As soon as the food has frozen, she lifts it out of the casserole, wraps it in heavy freezer foil, then returns it to the freezer. At party time, her work is done. She just removes the foil, slips the frozen blocks back into the casseroles, and heats them. A grand idea.

Curry-Favor Casserole (8 servings)

Here's one of the easiest, tastiest, and surest-to-please casseroles you can serve to guests who enjoy curry. Prepare in the morning, keeping the sauce separate till serving time.

For each portion, allow 1 slice of baked ham cut 1/4 inch thick. Trim off fat and place ham in a large shallow casserole, or in individual baking dishes. Cover ham with hard-cooked egg, halved, or a broiled or sautéed, boned breast of chicken, or a 1/4-inch-thick slice breast of turkey, or a boiled sweetbread, floured and browned in melted butter. Make 2 cups Cream of Curry Sauce (see recipe) or use 1 can (10 1/2-ounce) cream of mushroom soup and cream or evaporated milk to make 2 cups, add 1 teaspoon or more of curry and other seasonings to taste, and cook to blend flavors well.

Just before serving, pour sauce into casserole or baking dishes over ham and other meat, sprinkle generously with about 1 cup grated Parmesan or Swiss cheese mixed with 1/4 cup freshly-made butter-cracker crumbs. Place in a moderate oven, 350° F., to heat through, 15 to 20 minutes. (Individual dishes will take only 10 to 12 minutes to heat.) Raise to 400° *after* casserole gets hot. When sauce bubbles and crumbs brown, your delectable dish is ready to serve and curry favor.

Cassoulet from Carcassonne (8 servings)

You can prepare this cassoulet a day ahead except for the baking. Slip it into the oven about 1 1/2 hours before serving time. It's easy to keep it hot for a long time on a warming plate on the buffet.

1 pound sage-flavored pork sausage links
2 cloves garlic, sliced
3 pounds lean lamb, beef, or veal, cut in 1-inch chunks
3 onions, peeled and chopped
2 stalks celery with leaves, diced
2 tablespoons melted butter
Salt and pepper to taste
*1/4 teaspoon Sensation Seasoner**
*1/4 teaspoon Kitchen Spice**
2 1/2 cups tomatoes
1 teaspoon sugar
1/8 teaspoon basil
1/8 teaspoon thyme
1 bay leaf
2 tablespoons minced parsley
Dash soy sauce
1 to 2 cups consommé or more
1 pound dried navy or Great Northern beans soaked overnight and cooked until tender or 2 (1-pound) cans kidney beans with liquor
1 cup buttered crumbs

Fry sausage until done but not hard, drain, cut in 1-inch pieces, and set aside. Add garlic, meat, onions, celery, butter, and seasonings. Cook until meat is no longer rare and vegetables are soft—10 to 15 minutes. Stir occasionally to keep from sticking. Mix tomatoes with sugar, herbs, and soy sauce. Taste and correct seasonings.

To make the cassoulet, grease a deep casserole or bean pot with butter or drippings. Arrange alternate layers of beans and sausage, topped with a layer of the meat-and-onion mixture, a layer of tomatoes, then beans, until all ingredients are used up. Pour enough consommé so you can see the liquid, but do not cover the food. Add more later if needed. (The cooked cassoulet should be *moist,* neither runny nor dry.) Cover and set casserole in a moderate oven, 350° F. As soon as casserole is hot increase to 400°. Let cook 45 minutes to 1 hour. Uncover, sprinkle with buttered crumbs and bake another 15 minutes or until crumbs brown and meat is very tender. Then bring to buffet.

Paella Valenciana (8 servings)

This is my candidate for Queen of Meal-in-One Dishes, wonderful for a "Spanish" cocktail-supper. We ate the best in Madrid at the Palace Hotel. It was served in a special, two-handled, round baking dish of hand-forged copper, but any 2- to 3-inch-deep casserole will do. Use two, if you need to, for eight servings. Here's the recipe I adapted for American tables with a base of Saffron Rice. Spaniards cook this as the Italians do spaghetti, leaving it a little chewy. For convenience, make a day ahead and refrigerate.

Saffron Rice

¼ cup olive oil (no substitutes)
2 cloves garlic, crushed
2 large onions, peeled and minced
2 cups rice
Dash red and black pepper
¼ teaspoon thyme
¼ teaspoon rosemary
½ teaspoon Spanish saffron
6 cups stock or consommé
Salt

Heat oil in a deep heavy skillet. Add garlic, onions, rice, and pepper. Cook until rice begins to brown, stirring constantly. Add other ingredients, salt last as broth may be salty. Cover, turn heat low as soon as mixture begins to boil. Simmer until rice is done, stirring occasionally—30 minutes or a little longer should do it. If, when rice is cooked, the mixture is runny, remove lid and cook until liquid evaporates. Stir once in a while.

Paella

2 cups any mixed cooked shellfish: shrimp, lobster bits, oysters, mussels, crabs
2 cups any mixed cooked vegetables: canned tiny artichokes, green peas, small green beans, baby butter beans
8 serving-sized pieces fried chicken, rabbit, or other game
4 broiled lobster tails, slivered, or 2 to 3 cups cooked shellfish
½ cup melted butter
Parsley

Correct seasoning and turn Saffron Rice mixed with shellfish and vegetables into the casserole. On top, arrange pieces of chicken or rabbit, etc., with the lobster or shellfish, and pour in melted butter. Place in a 400° F. oven to heat—15 to 20 minutes, but avoid cooking dry. Sprinkle with parsley and bring to the table.

Ragout of Lamb (8 servings)

At the Venta Aires Restaurant in Toledo, Spain, this was brought to the table in a covered pottery casserole (about 10 inches across and 3 deep). A mound of fragrant Saffron Rice (see above) accompanied it.

3 pounds lean lamb, cut from the leg into 1½-inch cubes
Salt
Freshly-ground black pepper
4 tablespoons flour
6 tablespoons olive oil
2 cups consommé or bouillon (about)
½ cup Spanish sherry
2 garlic cloves, mashed
3 tablespoons lime or lemon juice
3 tablespoons chopped parsley

Season the lamb generously with salt and pepper, dredge with flour, sauté in olive oil until browned all over. Stir in other ingredients, except juice and parsley, and heat. Then pour into casserole, cover, and set in a moderate oven, 350° F. Bake for 1 to 1½ hours, or until lamb is really tender. (Do not cook dry—add more consommé or bouillon if necessary.) Thicken gravy with a flour-and-water paste if it needs it. Just before serving, stir in lime or lemon juice and garnish with the parsley. Let each guest help himself to rice and top his portion generously with ragout. This can be kept warm a long time on a hot plate or over an alcohol burner. It suffers not a whit from standing.

Cornish Suet Crust (for 12 individual pies)

Buy white beef-kidney suet, free from meat or skin, and have it ground. This pastry is easy to handle and lends itself to endless shaping, rolling, and fluting; it is amazingly flaky and delicate after baking. It also freezes better, uncooked, than any pastry I have tried. I have made up English meat pies with it, wrapped them in foil, frozen them, and had them keep well for five to six months. I like individual foil pans or my own 1- by 2½- by 3-inch tart pans.

⅓ cup finely-ground beef-kidney suet, firmly packed
2 cups sifted flour
½ teaspoon baking powder
½ teaspoon salt
⅓ cup lard or vegetable shortening
6 to 8 tablespoons ice water
1 egg yolk or white mixed with 2 teaspoons cold water for glazing

Let suet stand until it is at room temperature. Sift flour, baking powder, and salt together. Add suet and lard or vegetable shortening. Mix with the fingers as for any other pastry. Add ice water—just enough to hold dough together. (It should be firm enough to roll but not dry or crumbly.) Roll out ⅛ to ¼ inch thick. It will look just like any other pastry but prove more "durable."

Cut out rounds to fit your pie or muffin pans, line with the pastry. Spoon in the meat of your choice, filling ⅔ full. Arrange top rounds of pastry slitting them to permit escape of steam. For a pretty touch, cut out a design with a vegetable cutter or even a thimble. Seal and trim top and bottom rounds. Brush with beaten egg-and-water mixture, and bake as indicated in the recipes which follow. The little pies look all the more appetizing if you stick a few sprigs of parsley in the center of each at serving time.

Old English Beefsteak-and-Kidney Pies, Sportsman's Choice (10 to 12 pies)

This is the finest of all English meat pies; use only *young* veal kidneys, as they do in Penzance in Cornwall.

4 young veal kidneys
¼ cup butter or margarine
1 pound lean top round or sirloin tip steak
1 clove garlic, crushed
2 onions, peeled and diced
½ pound fresh mushrooms, slivered
3 cups water
1 tablespoon Worcestershire
½ teaspoon Kitchen Bouquet or Browning *
½ teaspoon B.V. paste or 1 bouillon cube
½ teaspoon soy sauce
Salt, pepper, seasoning salt
Flour
¼ cup minced parsley
¼ cup sherry or more
1 teaspoon French cognac or domestic brandy
1 recipe Cornish Suet Crust

To prepare kidneys, cut lobes away from white tubes, *removing any adhering white skin.* This is tedious, but most important for flavor. Rinse pieces of kidney well and drain. Melt butter or margarine in a deep skillet or Dutch oven. Brown steak on both sides but do not cook through. Remove from pan. Brown kidneys lightly and as they begin to turn color, add garlic, onions, and mushrooms. Cook until vegetables are soft, but not browned. Add water, steak, and other ingredients except flour, liquors, and parsley. Cover and simmer until meat is very tender—about an hour. Or cook in a pressure cooker 15 pounds' pressure 15 minutes.

Remove steak, trim off all fat, cut meat into bite-sized pieces. Thicken gravy with a paste of 2 tablespoons flour and 2 of water for each cup liquid. Correct seasoning, add parsley, liquors. Spoon mixture into 12 small pastry-lined pans to ⅔ full. Arrange top pastry, slit, trim, glaze, and bake in a hot oven, 450° F., until golden and well done, 30 to 40 minutes. If dry, pour in extra gravy through a funnel.

Hunt Breakfast Porkie Pies (12 small pies)

This is my adaptation of the classic British Melton Mobray Pork Pie. Serve hot or cold, as the British prefer.

1 pig's foot, split, or 1 large veal knuckle
3 pounds lean tenderloin pork
3 onions, peeled and minced
1 clove garlic, minced
Salt and pepper
1 teaspoon Sensation Seasoner or seasoning salt*
*¼ teaspoon Kitchen Spice **
¼ cup butter or margarine
3 sprigs fresh thyme or ¼ teaspoon powdered thyme

3 sprigs parsley
1 leaf sage or ¼ teaspoon powdered sage
1 stalk celery with leaves
4 cups water (about)
¼ teaspoon soy sauce
¼ teaspoon M.S.G.
4 tablespoons flour
3 tablespoons minced parsley
½ pound mushrooms (optional)
2 tablespoons butter (optional)
1 recipe Cornish Suet Crust

Put left column of ingredients into pressure cooker. Brown pork, turn once, stir vegetables occasionally. Pour off excess fat. Add all ingredients except flour, minced parsley, mushrooms, and butter. Cover and cook at 15 pounds' pressure 45 minutes to 1 hour (the tenderloin will take less time than tougher cuts). The pork should be falling to pieces and tender as butter. Or use a Dutch oven or deep skillet. Cut meat in small pieces. Proceed as above, adding more water if needed. Cover and simmer about 3 hours.

Pour off broth, reserve 2 cups and add flour. Beat until thick in a blender or mix a little flour to form a paste and add to hot broth. Cook until thick. Add parsley. Discard bones. Cut meat into ½-inch pieces (if not already so). If including mushrooms, chop fine, sauté in butter or pork drippings, then mix with meat. Fill pastry-lined pans ⅔ full. Top, trim, glaze, and bake in a hot oven, 450° F., for ½ hour or until crust is a glorious brown.

Palace Royal Lamb Pies (for 12 pies)

These small meat pies, said to have been great favorites of British royalty, often appeared for afternoon tea at Windsor Castle and Buckingham Palace. Certainly they are delicious means to a wonderful party dish from leftover lamb.

3 cups cooked ground lamb
1½ tablespoons minced parsley
6 large mushrooms, ground
2 onions, peeled and minced
Salt and black pepper
2 teaspoons Worcestershire sauce
1½ cups highly-seasoned gravy
1 recipe Cornish Suet Crust

Mix all ingredients (but pastry) until moist but not runny. Line 12 small pans with pastry and fill each ⅔ full with mixture. Arrange top pastry, brush with beaten-egg mixture, and bake in a hot oven, 450° F., until tops brown and pastry is well done, about 30 minutes.

Ham and Veal Pies (12 small pies)

Ever since Dickens published *Pickwick Papers,* the lovable Sam Weller has made the literary world aware of "'am and weal" pies. Wouldn't you and your guests like to try one?

2 pounds veal cutlet (from leg)
Salt and pepper
¼ teaspoon nutmeg
⅛ teaspoon mace
*¼ teaspoon Sensation Seasoner * or seasoning salt*
4 tablespoons butter or margarine
1 onion, peeled and minced
2 cups water (about)
1 thin strip lemon peel
1 cup diced baked ham, fat removed
1 hard-cooked egg, chopped
⅓ teaspoon mixed dried tarragon, thyme, marjoram
2 tablespoons chopped parsley
½ cup slivered fresh mushrooms or 3-ounce can broiled mushrooms, drained (optional)
½ cup oysters (optional)
½ cup diced boiled sweetbreads (optional)
Butter (optional)
4 tablespoons flour (about)
1 recipe Cornish Suet Crust

Sprinkle veal with seasonings, place in pressure cooker or Dutch oven where butter or margarine has been melted. Brown on one side. Turn, add onion, brown other side. Pour off excess fat and reserve. Add 2 cups water and lemon peel to pressure cooker, cook 15 to 20 minutes at 15 pounds' pressure, until meat is tender. Or add 3 to 4 cups water to Dutch oven, cover, and cook 50 minutes to an hour.

Strain off broth. Measure 2 cups (if not enough add water). Cut veal into ½-inch cubes. Mix ham, egg, herbs, and parsley in with veal. If using mushrooms, oysters, and sweetbreads, sauté in 3 tablespoons reserved fat or butter until well heated and edges of oysters curl—3 or 4 minutes—season with salt and pepper and add to meat. Mix flour with a little cold water, add to broth. Pour over ham-and-veal mixture, cook, stirring constantly until gravy thickens. Spoon into pastry-lined pans or ramekins, filling ⅔ full. Top with pastry, trim, and glaze. Bake about ½ hour in a hot oven, 450° F., until top browns and sides are done.

Note: If optional ingredients are added, 2 to 4 extra pies can be made.

12 WITH A FINE ITALIAN HAND

No more tempting dishes exist than pastas, and none can compare with those perfected over a period of centuries by fine Italian hands. The term *pasta* is often confusing since it refers to cooky and pastry dough as well as unsweetened dough used for spaghetti, macaroni, noodles, and such. In this chapter we are only concerned with the last group.

There are hundreds of these pastas from hair-thin spaghetti to thick tufoli—a giant macaroni-like tube which can be stuffed. There is a limitless variety of shapes—wide strips or broad flat ribbons called lasagne, bowknots, little hats, shells, ruffles, and so on. Many of these are available commercially now; try them in some of these main-dish pastas which follow.

The pasta casseroles can be prepared a long time ahead. Cover with foil and freeze until ready to use. Then heat in a moderate (350° F.) oven until hot and bubbling. Or refrigerate until time to heat for serving.

Lasagne Zurla à la Leoni (4 servings)

Here is a wonderful recipe for lasagne from my friend P. G. Leoni, proprietor of one of the outstanding European eating houses, the famous Quo Vadis Restaurant in London.

Put an 8-ounce package of green spinach noodles (lasagne verdi) in 3 quarts boiling water. Use a large kettle. Add salt and a teaspoon oil to keep noodles from sticking. Cook about 7 to 10 minutes, depending on how *chewy* you like your pasta. Let stand in water until ready to combine with the two sauces, then drain well.

Leoni's White Sauce:

½ cup butter or margarine
1 rounded tablespoon flour
1 cup milk
Salt and black pepper
2 tablespoons heavy cream or evaporated milk

Melt fat in a skillet. Add flour and mix to a paste. Add milk slowly; stir constantly. Season, pour in cream or evaporated milk and continue stirring until thickened.

Leoni's Meat-and-Tomato Sauce:

6 tablespoons leaf lard or other fat
½ pound cooked ground beef, veal, or chicken
1 large onion, peeled and minced
1 cup water (about)
Salt and black pepper
¼ teaspoon sugar
2 tablespoons Italian tomato paste, or other paste plus ⅛ teaspoon dried basil
Flour, if needed

Melt fat in skillet. Add meat and onion and stir until browned. Add water to cover and other ingredients. Bring to a boil. Cover, reduce heat, simmer until mixture thickens—about 20 to 30 minutes. If not the consistency of a thin cream sauce, add a little flour, first mixed to a paste with water.

Now place a layer of cooked noodles in the bottom of buttered casserole. Cover with a layer of Leoni's White Sauce, add a layer of grated Parmesan cheese (or substitute Swiss), then a layer of Leoni's Meat-and-Tomato Sauce. Repeat layers, ending with grated cheese on top. Put in a moderate oven, 375° F., until hot and cheese melts—20 to 30 minutes. Then serve.

Note: For convenience, prepare sauces and lasagne ahead; refrigerate, or wrap in foil and freeze prepared casserole.

In-a-Hurry Lasagne (8 servings)

This recipe has five main parts, but don't be discouraged! It is one of the easiest company dishes I know. Make the lasagne a day ahead and refrigerate. Half an hour before you are to serve, just reheat it in the oven.

Part I:

1 whole chicken in a can, weighing 2¼ to 2½ pounds
1 to 1½ cups chicken broth
2 tablespoons flour
¼ teaspoon soy sauce
Salt and black pepper
¼ cup minced parsley
¼ teaspoon M.S.G. (optional)

Drain chicken. Remove skin and bones, leaving chicken in as large pieces as possible. Do not handle more than necessary as it flakes easily.

In-a-Hurry Lasagne

Part II:

Prepare chicken gravy. Measure broth from can, mix a little with flour to form a paste, then gradually stir in rest. Add other ingredients and cook over low heat, stirring until thickened.

Part III:

Prepare Italian Meatless Tomato Sauce (see recipe).

Part IV:

Boil ½ pound lasagne, or the widest noodles available, in salted water about 10 minutes, or until done but chewy. Drain well.

Part V:

Cut into 8 thin slices ½ pound Mozzarella or Swiss cheese and have on hand ½ cup Parmesan or grated Swiss cheese for sprinkling on top.

With the five parts assembled, you are ready to make the lasagne. In a large casserole, put a little chicken gravy, a layer of noodles, one of cheese slices, then a layer of chicken followed by tomato sauce. Now noodles again, chicken gravy, cheese, chicken meat, and tomato sauce, until all ingredients have been used. Top layer should be noodles. Refrigerate.

Half an hour before serving, sprinkle on the ½ cup grated cheese, pop the lasagne into a 375° F. oven and when bubbly and top is browned, bring to the table. Your guests will be delighted.

Noodles and Sausage, the Spanish way (12 servings)

The Spaniards have a way with pastas too. This recipe is one of the best buffet dishes for the busy hostess to serve. Cook the casserole ahead, refrigerate or freeze, and reheat when ready. Also it makes a very inexpensive main dish.

1 pound sage-flavored pork sausage
2 tablespoons olive oil
1 pound fresh mushrooms or 2 (6-ounce) cans broiled mushrooms
4 large onions, peeled and minced
2 cloves garlic, crushed
2 green peppers, minced (seeds removed)
*1 teaspoon Kitchen Bouquet or Browning **
2 tablespoons Worcestershire sauce
½ teaspoon paprika
½ teaspoon saffron
¼ teaspoon black pepper
6 drops Tabasco
Salt
2 bay leaves
¼ teaspoon each: basil, marjoram, rosemary
5 to 6 cups condensed tomato soup
1 pound ½-inch-wide noodles, boiled and drained
1 cup sliced stuffed olives
1 cup grated Parmesan or Swiss cheese (optional)

Fry sausage in a Dutch oven, stirring constantly. When brown and crumbly but not hard, remove, drain, and put aside. Add olive oil to fat in pot, and the fresh mushrooms if you are using them. Cover and cook 10 minutes. Mix in onions, garlic, green peppers, seasonings, and herbs. Cook 10 minutes, stirring occasionally. Add sausage and canned mushrooms with liquor if using them instead of fresh. Pour in soup and simmer 10 minutes longer until vegetables are done. Add noodles and olives. Heat and pour into a deep bowl or tureen. Dust with grated cheese or serve plain.

Note: Use saffron made from stamens of saffron crocus, not the dried leaf sort. The latter has a medicinal taste.

Florentine Cannelloni with Cheese Sauce (6 servings)

Use broad (2½- to 3-inch) noodles or lasagne. Drop ½ pound, a few at a time, in a large kettle of boiling salted water. Cook 5 to 7 minutes or until chewy but not raw. Drain. Cut into 4- to 5-inch lengths, wipe dry, spread each piece with a tablespoon of this:

½ pound mushrooms
1 small clove garlic, minced
3 tablespoons olive oil
1 cup cooked ground chicken
1 hard-cooked egg, riced
⅛ teaspoon thyme
⅛ teaspoon rosemary
1 or 2 tablespoons cream
Salt and pepper

Grind mushrooms and garlic together; brown lightly in hot oil. Add other ingredients (enough cream to moisten) and mix. Cool slightly and spread on cannelloni. Roll up like a little muff. Place side by side, only one layer deep, in a casserole or in individual baking dishes, allowing 2 to a person. Cover with:

Cheese Sauce:

2 tablespoons butter
2 tablespoons flour
1 cup chicken broth
½ cup heavy cream or evaporated milk
Salt and pepper
½ cup grated Parmesan or Romano cheese
Extra cheese for topping

Melt butter, stir in flour to form a smooth paste. Add broth slowly, stirring all the while, then cream or milk, and seasonings. Cook until medium thick. Add cheese and pour sauce over cannelloni. Top with more grated cheese.

Near serving time, set cannelloni in a cold broiler, not too near flame. Broil until mixture is heated through, top is browned, and cheese melted. Serve very hot.

Cannelloni with Tomato Sauce

For the chicken filling, substitute 1 cup cooked ground ham or veal, or ½ pound chicken livers, sautéed in butter with a peeled chopped onion, and ground. Use Italian Meatless Tomato Sauce (see recipe) instead of Cheese Sauce. Prepare as directed above.

Chicken Livers and Mushroom Spaghetti (8 servings)

This is a delightful dish and one which can be made quickly.

½ pound sliced breakfast bacon
1 pound fresh chicken livers, or frozen, defrosted
¼ cup bacon drippings or olive oil (about)
1 pound fresh mushrooms
2 large onions, peeled and diced
4 cups Italian Meatless Tomato Sauce (see recipe)
Salt and pepper
Dash soy sauce
¼ teaspoon M.S.G.
2 pounds spaghetti, cooked and drained
Grated Parmesan cheese

Fry bacon until crisp and brown. Drain, then crumble. Sauté the washed, drained livers in bacon drippings or oil. Cook covered until livers stop popping; stir occasionally. Uncover and brown, then remove livers. Sauté mushrooms and onions using more fat if needed. Add tomato sauce, seasonings, return livers to sauce and cook thoroughly.

Serve spaghetti in a tureen. Place chicken livers and mushrooms in a deep bowl, sprinkle with bacon. Have a bowl of grated cheese beside the spaghetti. Let each guest help himself to a soup plate of spaghetti, a ladle full of sauce, and a good sprinkling of cheese.

Stuffed Tufoli (8 servings)

Drop 16 tufoli (about 1 pound) into large kettle of boiling salted water, with a little oil added. Cook until just tender, not too done, about 10 minutes, since they are going to be cooked again. Drain; be careful not to split tubes. When cool, stuff as follows:

1 pound dry cottage cheese or ricotta
1 egg
1 onion, peeled and minced
4 shallots and tops, minced
2 tablespoons olive oil or butter
½ cup chopped salted almonds or pecans
2 tablespoons minced parsley
2 tablespoons ground Italian salami, prosciutto, or baked ham
Salt and pepper
Dash Worcestershire sauce
Dash soy sauce
¼ teaspoon M.S.G.
8 thin slices Mozzarella or Swiss cheese
4 cups Italian Meatless Tomato Sauce (see recipe)
Grated Parmesan or Romano cheese

Beat cottage cheese or ricotta with an electric mixer or use a strong right arm. Add egg, onion, shallots sautéed 3 minutes in oil or butter, nuts, parsley, meat, and seasonings. Poke mixture gently into tufoli, plumping them out as much as possible and stuffing from both ends—not too full or tubes will burst when cooked again. Place side by side, one layer deep, in large, shallow, copper baking dishes. Or use individual baking dishes, putting 2 tufoli in each.

Place a slice of cheese over every 2 tufoli. Pour on a thin layer of tomato sauce, sprinkle freely with grated cheese. Bake in a 350° F. oven, 20 to 30 minutes, until sauce bubbles and cheese browns. Or run under broiler at the last minute to brown well. Prepare ahead if you wish (except for grated cheese on top), refrigerate, or wrap in foil and freeze. Then bake when ready to use.

Italian Meatless Tomato Sauce (4 cups)

This is the tomato sauce served everywhere in Italy over pastas, vegetables, and meats.

No. 2½ can peeled Italian tomatoes
2 small garlic cloves, minced
2 sprigs thyme
1 teaspoon sugar
⅛ teaspoon cayenne
3 tablespoons olive oil
Few needles rosemary
Few leaves basil
1 teaspoon salt, or more
Flour (optional)

Place all ingredients in a saucepan, cover, and simmer 20 minutes or until mixture is as thick as tomato purée. Stir occasionally to keep from sticking. Strain, or put through food mill, or whip in blender. Store, covered, in refrigerator. Use as needed. If you want a thicker sauce, add 1 tablespoon flour, mixed with 2 tablespoons water, for every cup purée. Cook 2 minutes stirring constantly.

Note: Other tomatoes can be used but Italian tomatoes have a distinctive flavor. Substitute a No. 2 can tomatoes, a 6-ounce can tomato paste, and 3 cans water.

13 THEY FLEW THE COOP

Both fresh and frozen poultry are always plentiful, and often the cheapest meat on the market. Chicken has universal appeal and it's a safe choice for the main dish when you aren't familiar with your guests' preferences. In this chapter you'll find many easy ways to prepare it. Some of the recipes are unusual specialties; others, old favorites which my family and friends have enjoyed.

Breasts of Chicken with Sour Cream and Mushrooms (8 servings)

8 breasts chicken
1 carrot, scraped and cut in rings
1 onion, peeled and diced
Salt and pepper
2 sprigs parsley
2 shallots, diced
2 stalks celery with leaves, diced
¼ teaspoon soy sauce
*¼ teaspoon Sensation Seasoner * or seasoning salt*
2 cups water or more

Place chicken breasts—preferably boned—in a roasting pan with other ingredients. Cover and cook until very tender, about 1 hour in a 350° F. oven. Pour off gravy. Strain. (There should be 2 cups.)

Sour-Cream Mushroom Sauce:

A most delicious and unusual sauce; one to serve often.

2 cloves garlic, pressed
1 pound fresh mushrooms
6 tablespoons butter
Salt and pepper
¼ cup flour
2 cups chicken broth
1 cup sour cream

Place garlic and mushrooms in a wooden bowl and chop fine. Melt butter. Stir in mushroom mixture and season. Cover and cook 3 or 4 minutes over low heat. Stir occasionally. Add flour mixed to a paste with broth and cook until thick, stirring constantly. Pour in sour cream. Keep heat low. Stir until hot; watch carefully not to let it boil and curdle. *High heat often causes the sauce to separate.*

To serve, place chicken breasts on a platter and either pour sauce over them or pass separately. This sauce can be kept warm on a hot plate or in a chafing dish.

Note: Cornish squab chickens can be prepared the same way.

Madras Curried Spring Chickens (8 servings)

This is one of the simplest chicken recipes I know—and one of the best.

4 spring chickens, halved
1 cup butter or part margarine
Salt and black pepper
2 to 4 tablespoons curry powder
8 onions, peeled and diced
3 cups water
¼ cup chopped parsley
Paprika
2 tablespoons lime or lemon juice

Place chickens in melted butter or margarine in a roaster. You may have to cook a few at a time. Dust with salt, pepper, and half the curry. Brown lightly on each side; do not cook until done. Sauté onions until soft. Add rest of curry and water. This part can be done in the morning.

About an hour or so before serving time, put roaster, covered, in a 350° F. oven. Bake chickens until tender, about an hour. Place chickens on a large mound of boiled rice, sprinkle with parsley, and dust with paprika. Add lime or lemon juice to unthickened broth and serve in a separate bowl. Your guests help themselves to chicken and rice, and douse the gravy over all. (Don't be upset if butter comes to top. Just mix it up between servings.)

Chicken Abbott (8 servings)

Mary Snow and Bud Abbott are as well known for their fine food as for their lively radio and television programs in Louisville. Here's one of the specialties of their very charming house, a most unusual chicken dish to serve with noodles.

8 boned chicken breasts
1 cup olive oil (no substitutes)
1 cup Lea and Perrins Worcestershire sauce
Salt and black pepper
1 tablespoon Kitchen Bouquet
1 teaspoon curry powder or more
1 teaspoon fresh tarragon or ¼ teaspoon dried
1 teaspoon fresh rosemary or ¼ teaspoon dried

Marinate chicken breasts in all ingredients for at least 3 hours. Place side by side in a roasting pan and pour on marinade. Cover and bake in a moderate oven, 350° F., 50 minutes to 1 hour, or until chicken is very tender. Just before bringing to the table, run chicken under broiler long enough to brown each side. Serve with boiled noodles sprinkled lightly with caraway seeds. Use pan gravy to moisten both noodles and chicken.

Squabs, Korean Style (8 servings)

8 squabs or small boned chickens
½ cup soy or shoyu sauce
1 tablespoon sugar or honey
¼ teaspoon black and red pepper mixed
2-inch piece fresh ginger, peeled and sliced, or 1 teaspoon ground ginger
¼ cup sesame or olive oil
2 small onions, peeled and grated
2 garlic cloves, crushed
1 tablespoon Worcestershire sauce
½ cup gin
Salt, if needed

Soak squabs or chickens all day or overnight in the above marinade. To cook, follow directions for Chicken Abbott (recipe above) and serve with fluffy rice.

Chicken and Chestnuts (8 servings)

This flavorful eighteenth-century recipe, a meat-and-vegetable course all in one, should be served when you can get the large Italian or Japanese chestnuts. Allow half a chicken to each person.

4 spring chickens, split (about 1¾ pounds each)
1 cup melted butter or part margarine
Salt and black pepper
2 cups boiling water
*¼ teaspoon each: nutmeg, mace, cloves, or ¾ teaspoon Kitchen Spice**
6 cups cooked peeled chestnuts
¼ cup diced celery
¼ cup scraped diced carrots
8 shallots and tops, minced
Juice of 1 lemon
¼ cup chopped parsley
Flour

Place chickens side by side in broiler. Brush with butter or margarine, sprinkle with salt and pepper, brown on each side, basting occasionally. Transfer to a casserole. Add boiling water to drippings and pour over chickens. Then add in other ingredients except parsley and flour. Cover and bake in a 350° F. oven for 1 hour or until chickens are tender. Gravy can be thickened with a flour-and-water paste if desired. Sprinkle chickens with parsley. Bring piping-hot casserole to the table.

Note: A quick, easy way to peel chestnuts. Put 1 pound at a time in a pressure cooker with 2 cups water. Cook 10 minutes at 15 pounds' pressure. The inside skin then comes off with the shell. Otherwise cover with water and boil 30 minutes.

Arroz con Pollo (8 servings)
(Spanish Chicken with Saffron Rice)

Don't be fooled by the foreign title. This is merely old-fashioned fricasseed chicken served over a mound of delicious Saffron Rice (see recipe). Here's how to prepare the chicken.

2 three-pound chickens, quartered
Salt and pepper
½ cup flour
½ cup peanut oil or lard
2 cloves garlic, minced
3 (10-ounce) packages frozen peas, cooked
Tiny canned artichokes for garnish

Roll pieces of chicken in well-seasoned flour. Fry in hot fat until golden brown but not cooked through. Transfer to another pan. Pour off excess fat, saving browned crumbs. Add 4 cups water, garlic, and additional salt and pepper. Bring to boiling. Return chicken, let liquid come to a boil again, then lower heat. Cover and cook slowly for about 2 hours or until chicken is tender and gravy thick. Don't let it burn. Add more water if gravy cooks too low. (Or cook 45 to 50 minutes in a pressure cooker at 15 pounds' pressure.)

To serve this mouth-watering chicken, pile a mound of Saffron Rice on a large platter. Arrange golden-brown pieces of chicken on top. Surround with green peas in pretty paper muffin cups (or in timbales) and tiny artichokes. Serve the rich gravy in a separate bowl.

Tidewater Chicken-and-Sweetbread Croquettes
(8 large croquettes)

These croquettes are an adaptation of a recipe from colonial Virginia. They can be made up and breaded, then wrapped in freezer foil and frozen. When ready to use, fry the unthawed croquettes in deep fat until golden. Place on a foil-lined pan in a 325° F. oven until heated through. Transfer the pan to a warming plate on your buffet table. The croquettes will remain hot until ready to serve. Try them—they're terrific!

2 tablespoons chicken fat or butter
1 onion, peeled and grated
2 rounded tablespoons flour
1 cup chicken or sweetbread broth
2 teaspoons Worcestershire sauce
1/8 teaspoon black pepper
1/4 teaspoon soy or Maggi sauce
1/4 teaspoon nutmeg
Salt to taste
1/4 teaspoon seasoning salt
2 eggs
1/2 cup heavy cream or evaporated milk
2 cups ground cooked chicken
1 cup ground boiled sweetbreads
1/2 ounce cracker crumbs (about 2 tablespoons)
3 tablespoons minced parsley
Freshly-made bread crumbs
Deep fat for frying
1 tablespoon butter

Melt chicken fat or butter, brown onion slightly, add flour and stir until smooth and dark brown but not burned. Pour in broth slowly and add all seasonings. Cook until thick. Cool slightly, then add egg yolks beaten with cream or milk. Pour over chicken, sweetbreads, and cracker crumbs. (I prefer butter to soda crackers for this.) Add parsley. Cook mixture in skillet until no longer runny and a paste begins to form which leaves sides of pan when stirred. *Do not cook dry.* This is important. Put in a bowl, cover, and refrigerate overnight or until very cold, before shaping croquettes.

To make the croquettes: Roll a heaping tablespoon of the chicken-sweetbread mixture into a ball, then shape into an oblong. Roll in bread crumbs, in egg whites beaten slightly with a tablespoon of cold water, and again in crumbs. Fry in deep fat (with the tablespoon butter added) 375° F. about 3 minutes. Or you can cook croquettes in shallow inch-deep fat as I often do, browning on all sides. Drain on absorbent paper. Serve with any sauce you wish. I'm partial to:

Brown Sherry Sauce:

This is one of the most useful sauces in my files. It is delicious on anything—the sort, to quote Brillat-Savarin, "you could eat on your grandmother." With it, leftovers can be made into a party dish. Croquettes, broiled sweetbreads, chicken, shrimp, hard-cooked eggs, mushrooms, all taste wonderful with this sauce.

2 tablespoons butter (no substitutes)
¼ cup flour
3 cups stock
1 tablespoon Worcestershire sauce
1 tablespoon catsup
¼ teaspoon paprika
1 teaspoon Kitchen Bouquet
2 to 3 tablespoons minced parsley
½ cup heavy cream or evaporated milk
3 tablespoons sherry or more

Cook butter and flour until browned. Add stock, stirring constantly over low heat until thick. Add other ingredients except cream or milk and sherry. Cover and simmer slowly for 20 minutes. Add cream or milk and sherry. Cover and simmer about 10 minutes longer. Stir occasionally to prevent sticking. Correct seasoning and serve.

This can be made ahead. Reheat, and just before serving, taste and add more sherry if needed.

Variation: For Mushroom-and-Brown-Sherry Sauce, sauté ½ pound slivered, fresh mushrooms 3 or 4 minutes in 2 tablespoons melted butter. Fold into sauce about 5 minutes before sending to the table.

Chicken Terrapin (8 servings)

This used to be a favorite after-theater supper dish fifty years ago when such suppers were fashionable. It should come into its own again at present-day cocktail-suppers.

Bake or boil a 5- to 6-pound hen or a small turkey a day or two before using. Dice the meat, save the pan juices or stock for the sauce. Since this sauce tastes best cooked just before serving, make it in your chafing dish right at the buffet.

3 tablespoons butter
2 tablespoons flour
2 cups stock
2 cups cream or evaporated milk
Salt and pepper
1 teaspoon Made Mustard * *or English mustard*
1/8 teaspoon M.S.G.
1/8 teaspoon cloves
1/4 teaspoon grated nutmeg
1/2 teaspoon sugar
1/4 teaspoon cayenne
1/4 teaspoon paprika
4 hard-cooked eggs, chopped
3 cups cooked diced chicken (about)
1/2 cup Madeira or sherry

Melt butter, add flour and stir to make a paste. Slowly add stock and cream or milk. Cook until thick, stirring constantly. Place over hot water. Add seasonings and eggs. Fold in chicken, add wine and mix well. This elegant chicken is sure to please your guests.

Variations: Substitute 3 cups boiled, diced sweetbreads for chicken. Or you can extend the recipe with a cup of oysters sautéed until plump in a tablespoon of butter, mixed in when you add the chicken. Or sauté a pound of fresh mushrooms in butter 5 minutes, then make the sauce as directed.

Turkey Hodgepodge (8 servings)

This is a recipe I often use for cocktail-suppers. It can't be beat for goodness and economy and it freezes well. Heat and serve over rice, noodles, or in patty shells.

4 cups cooked turkey, cut in 1-inch pieces
½ cup chicken fat, butter, or margarine
1 cup diced celery
1¼ cups diced peeled onions
2 garlic cloves, mashed
1 cup chopped green peppers
2 fresh or canned pimientos, chopped
¼ teaspoon each: black pepper, soy sauce, M.S.G., curry powder
*1 teaspoon Sensation Seasoner**
1 teaspoon Worcestershire sauce
1 bouillon cube or ½ teaspoon B.V. paste
1½ to 2 cups stock
1 cup milk (or half milk, half cream)
½ cup flour
2 tablespoons minced celery leaves
2 tablespoons minced parsley

Make sauce for turkey in a Dutch oven or deep saucepan. Melt the fat. Add celery, onions, garlic, green peppers, and *fresh* pimientos. (If canned ones are used, add them later.) Simmer slowly until vegetables are soft, stirring occasionally, about 10 minutes. Mix in seasonings and bouillon or B.V. paste. Slowly stir liquids (mixed to a smooth paste with the flour) into vegetables, stirring with a wooden spoon. Fold turkey in along with celery leaves and parsley. (Add *canned* pimientos now.) Taste for seasoning and serve. This can be kept hot indefinitely on a warming plate.

Note: Chicken can, of course, be used in place of turkey.

Broiled Smothered Turkey (Mock Pheasant) (6 servings)

The new Beltsville breed of turkey, when prepared this way, tastes a great deal like pheasant. For 6, have a 4½- to 6-pound turkey split down the back. Clean well, rinse, dry, salt and pepper freely inside and out, and brush with ½ cup melted butter or part margarine. Grill 6 inches from heat, brown on each side brushing occasionally with melted fat. When bird is golden brown, transfer to a large casserole or roasting pan with a lid, and pour over it:

1 cup white wine (about)
1 cup stock or consommé combined with pan drippings
1 clove garlic
1 small onion, peeled and sliced
2 sprigs fresh thyme or ¼ teaspoon dried
2 carrots, cut in rings
½ pound mushrooms
2 tablespoons butter or olive oil
2 tablespoons minced parsley
Salt and pepper
Flour
½ teaspoon sugar, if needed

Put wine, stock, garlic, onion, thyme, and carrots in casserole or roaster and set in a 350° F. oven. Cover. Bake 1 to 1½ hours, testing to see when tender. Do not let liquid cook away: add wine and water in equal proportions if necessary. Strain broth, add mushrooms sautéed in fat, and parsley. Thicken if you wish with flour mixed to a paste with a little water. If wine is very dry, add sugar.

Roast Goose (8 servings)

10-pound goose
2 cloves garlic
1 tablespoon salt
½ teaspoon black pepper
1 rounded teaspoon powdered ginger
3 cups water
Flour

Clean goose well. Mash together garlic, salt, pepper, and ginger. Rub goose inside and out with mixture. Let stand overnight. Prick skin on breast. Next day roast uncovered in a moderate oven, 350° F., until goose is brown all over, about 3 hours. Pour off all excess fat. Add water and cover. Cook until tender, 2 to 3 hours longer. (Goose takes from 30 to 40 minutes per pound.) Thicken broth with a flour-and-water paste. Cook a few minutes and serve. This roast goose is delicious hot or sliced cold.

Salmi of Goose (8 servings)

Sometime serve this gourmet hash rather than the whole goose at one of your cocktail-suppers. It can be made ahead and reheated; it also freezes well. Roast a day ahead, strain broth. Dice meat in inch pieces (there should be about 4 cups) and put in a covered bowl. Refrigerate.

Carcass and skin of goose
1 quart water
1 onion, peeled and sliced
1 clove garlic, sliced
1 allspice berry
1 whole clove
1 bay leaf
1 carrot, scraped and sliced
2 stalks celery with leaves, sliced
Salt and pepper
1 sprig parsley

Cook all ingredients in a pressure cooker at 15 pounds' pressure for 40 minutes. Or simmer in a soup kettle with about 2 quarts water 2 to 3 hours. Cool stock and strain.

Salmi Sauce for Goose:

½ cup butter
½ cup flour
4 cups well-seasoned stock
1 cup white wine
Salt and pepper
½ teaspoon sugar, if needed
4 cups diced goose
¼ cup minced parsley

Melt butter, add flour, and stir to a thick paste. Pour stock in slowly stirring all the while. (Use broth from roasting and from boiling carcass.) Add wine, salt, and pepper, and sugar if wine is dry. Mix in goose and heat thoroughly. Add parsley, correct seasoning, and serve over barley.

Pekin Duck (8 servings)

I ate ducks prepared this way at Shanghai Lil's Chinese restaurant in San Francisco and liked them so much I asked for the recipe. Your guests will too, after they have tried them. Marinate the ducks the day before your party.

2 four-pound ducks
1 cup strained honey
¼ cup boiling water
2 teaspoons salt
2 teaspoons soy sauce
2 teaspoons Chinese brown sauce or 2 more teaspoons soy sauce
2 ounces gin
2 teaspoons cornstarch

Brush ducks inside and out with marinade of above ingredients (except cornstarch). Place uncovered in refrigerator about 24 hours. Just before cooking brush once more. Pour off marinade. Roast uncovered in a 325° F. oven and baste every 20 minutes with marinade. It will take about 3½ hours for ducks to brown properly. Pour off all fat in roaster, add any marinade left and enough water to make 3 cups. (You may have to add more water later.) Cover and roast until ducks are tender, an hour or two longer. Strain broth. Add cornstarch mixed with a little cold water to about 2 cups broth. Cook over low heat 2 minutes, stirring constantly. Place ducks in serving dish, garnish with chopped parsley, and put a sauceboat of gravy beside them.

14 OF SAVORY MEAT

'Tis sweet to eat
When hunger's seat
Demands a treat
Of savory meat.
From an old book for children

When King Charles II landed in England after years of exile in France, the story goes that he stopped at a certain inn on the road to London and ordered dinner. Unfamiliar with the cut of beef served to him, he sent to the landlord to ask what it was. "Loin, Sire," he was told. Whereupon Charles, whose sense of humor must have been delightful, drew his sword, held it over the meat and solemnly pronounced, "I dub thee Sir Loin."

We can thank the British for plain grilled joints and roasts. French cooking tends to sauces and gravies rather than the rare roast beef of Old England or steak per se. One fashionable eighteenth-century London club was called *The Steaks*. Members met every Saturday, wore special uniforms and badges, and their number was limited to twenty-four males. Even the Prince Regent waited a year to join, and it was rumored he created a vacancy by sending a member to India. With such snob-appeal, no wonder the lesser citizens took up steak-eating with a vengeance.

Aspic of Beef Roularde, Duxelle (10 to 12 servings)

This old-world recipe is as impressive as its name, and one of the finest ways to serve cold roast beef I know. It is not a recipe to prepare on the spur of the moment, but the results are well worth the effort.

10- to 12-pound standing rib roast of beef
1 pound fresh mushrooms, ground
1 tablespoon chopped green pepper
1 onion, peeled and ground
1 shallot, ground
3 sprigs parsley, chopped
½ teaspoon mixed herbs: thyme, marjoram, tarragon
½ teaspoon seasoning salt
¼ teaspoon Kitchen Spice **
Salt
¼ teaspoon soy sauce
4 strips bacon
6 tablespoons olive oil
Juice of 1 lemon
2 cloves garlic, minced
1 tablespoon butter, if needed
Veal knuckle or 2 pig's feet, split
1 stalk celery and leaves, diced
1 tomato, peeled and sliced
1 carrot, scraped and sliced
2½ cups red wine
1 tablespoon tarragon vinegar
1 unpeeled onion (optional)
Gelatin, if needed

For the beef, mix together rest of ingredients in left column. Take to butcher. Have beef boned. Spread on mushroom stuffing, place bacon strips over it, and have butcher roll, skewer, and tie beef. (Bring home bones and trimmings.)

Marinate beef roll in olive oil, lemon juice, and garlic several hours or overnight. Then pour off marinade (reserve), wipe beef dry, and brown in roaster on top of stove. Use melted butter if necessary. Brown trimmings, bones, and veal knuckle or pig's feet. Add marinade, 1½ cups water, and remaining ingredients, except unpeeled onion and gelatin.

Place in a 350° F. oven and roast, covered, 2 to 3 hours depending on how rare you like beef. Do not cook until meat falls to pieces; it is to be served in slices. (I add a charred onion to my gravy for body and flavor, but it isn't essential. Bake a whole onion, skin and all, in a separate pan until dark brown and soft inside. Then mash into gravy.)

When meat is done, remove to a platter. Strain gravy, chill, and remove fat. Then spoon over beef until it coats and glazes it. Do this 24 to 48 hours before the party so aspic will jell properly. If necessary, for every 2 cups gravy, add 1 tablespoon gelatin softened in 2 tablespoons cold water and dissolved in 2 cups boiling gravy. Let chill and spoon over meat. Serve aspic of beef on the platter, garnish with parsley or water cress if you wish, and cut into thin slices. (If aspic falls from beef just scoop it up on the slice; it is delicious anyway!)

Fillet of Beef, Flambé (8 to 12 servings)

This is a most elegant recipe. The fillet can be prepared in advance with the final flamboyant touches added at the buffet table.

1 cup butter (no substitutes)
2 (2-ounce) cans imported pâté de foie gras with truffles
1 clove garlic, crushed
3- to 4-pound prime fillet of beef
Freshly-ground black pepper
Salt
¾ cup claret
1 tablespoon minced parsley
¼ cup brandy or bourbon whisky
12 large rounds of bread, buttered and sautéed until brown

Melt butter. Add pâté and garlic; mash to a paste, or whip in blender. Brush cold fillet of beef with warm butter mixture. It will form a hard coating. Sprinkle with pepper and refrigerate. Do this at least an hour before cooking.

Have broiler very hot. Place beef 3 inches from heat and cook 5 minutes. Salt broiled side, add half the claret, turn, and cook 5 minutes on the other side. Add rest of claret and sprinkle with salt. Turn meat and cook 5 more minutes on each side (20 minutes in all). Pour off juices and reserve.

To flame the fillet: Most hosts make a ritual of this. I make up a tray of ingredients and utensils I will need: a saucepan of hot pâté-wine mixture sprinkled with parsley, a glass of brandy or bourbon, a plate of sautéed bread rounds, and the fillet cut into inch-thick slices. Bring pâté-claret mixture to boiling, add brandy or bourbon. Touch a match to it, turn out the lights, and let it go to blue blazes. Tilt pan back and forth to keep flaming as long as possible. When flame dies, add several slices of meat. Just heat through. Each slice goes on a round of toast and gravy over it. Serve immediately. Guests will glady wait their turn. (You *could* heat all slices in a skillet in the kitchen, if you prefer.)

Dressed Beef Round (8 to 12 servings)

This recipe was given to me by my friend, Edith Campbell Bruce, one which she said had long been a Campbell specialty for company. It is, as far as I know, an absolutely original recipe from the Blue Grass of days gone by. Edith says this glorified pot roast appeals to men in particular and whenever she asks her three sons-in-law to a family party, they say, "We'll come if you have Dressed Beef Round."

8 to 12 pounds beef cut from the round
Cider vinegar
Salt and pepper
2 cups water
2 tablespoons walnut catsup
4 tablespoons Worcestershire sauce
½ cup sherry

The day before cooking, select a thick, not-too-wide, piece of beef. Have butcher lard it with fresh pork, cut deep gashes to hold dressing, tie, and trim well. Rub beef with vinegar. Stuff Special Dressing (recipe below) into slits and cover top and sides. Let season overnight.

To roast, place uncovered in a moderate oven, 350° F. Sprinkle with pepper and a little salt. (Dressing is salty.) Let brown all over, then add water, cover, and cook until tender—about 4 hours. Baste occasionally. Half an hour before serving, add walnut catsup and Worcestershire. (Thicken gravy if you want with a flour-and-water paste, though Edith doesn't.) Just before bringing to the table stir in sherry. Pass gravy separately. For a pretty effect garnish platter with parsley or water cress and orange slices with dabs of tart currant or plum jelly on them. When you slice the roast, you have a polka-dot effect.

Special Dressing for Dressed Beef Round

Since her family is so fond of this, Edith doubles the amount necessary to stuff and spread over the roast. The following recipe is the double amount; you can serve the extra instead of a starchy vegetable.

2 (1-pound) loaves white bread
2 large onions, peeled and sliced
2 cloves garlic
2 cups beef suet
4 carrots, scraped
½ cup sour pickles
*2 teaspoons Kitchen Spice * or mixed spices*
2 teaspoons celery seed
1 cup Crosse and Blackwell's mustard pickle
1 cup tomato sauce or catsup
½ cup chili sauce
2 tablespoons French mustard
Salt and pepper
Tabasco

Use day-old bread; leave uncovered overnight. Grind with finest blade of meat grinder. (If bread is too moist, dry in a 350° F. oven.) Grind onions, garlic, suet, carrots, and pickles if in large pieces. Add other ingredients. This should make a fairly stiff paste, but not dry. Mix in more tomato sauce or catsup if dry; or crumbs if wet.

Teriyaki Steak, Honolulu (8 servings)

For a glamorous summer cocktail-supper, prepare this steak over a charcoal grill out on the terrace. It makes a fine conversation piece. You can, of course, grill it under the broiler—less glamorous, but still delicious.

This recipe is a combination of two: one from Bert and Jo Biehl of Honolulu who first introduced me to Teriyaki Steak, and the other from Ralph and Shirley Bettman who gave me detailed instructions for cooking it. The marinade tenderizes the meat. You don't need *prime* beef; I've used *choice* with great success. I prefer a chubby sirloin cut, but if your grill is small, use two porterhouse steaks cut equally thick.

Teriyaki Steak, Honolulu (8 servings)

5½- to 6-pound sirloin cut 1½ to 1¾ inches thick
2-inch piece fresh ginger root or 2 teaspoons powdered
3 cloves garlic, crushed
3 tablespoons sugar
½ cup soy or shoyu sauce
1 ounce gin
1 cup butter or part margarine
Salt and pepper
1 ounce vermouth (optional)
Minced parsley (optional)
Minced shallots (optional)

Place sirloin in a shallow pan. Wash, peel, and sliver the ginger root. Mix with other ingredients in first column. (I whip these in a blender, but it is not essential.) Pour over meat. Do not cut down on sugar—3 tablespoons are needed. With a sharp-pronged fork, prick steak all over. Cover and refrigerate, turning every now and then. Soak overnight or at least 8 hours.

To cook, lift steak from its spicy bath and place over glowing charcoals (burned low). Cut fat from steak if you wish. Brown on each side, turning often to prevent too much charring. Grill 15 to 25 minutes depending on how rare you and your guests like it. When cooked enough, place in pan with marinade and melted butter, add salt and pepper to taste. Cook until sauce thickens slightly; turn meat once. Transfer steak to platter and cut into serving pieces. Add vermouth to bubbling sauce if you are using it. When hot, pour over meat. Sprinkle with parsley and shallots for garnish, but these ingredients are not necessary for flavor.

Kentucky Grilled Steak with Henry Bane Sauce (8 servings)

If you feel that Teriyaki Steak is too exotic, this is a fine alternate. Use same cut and size steak as above—but prime beef if you wish. Several hours before cooking, shower with freshly-ground black pepper. Grill as above. When cooked, add salt, and simmer steak a few minutes in 1 cup butter or part margarine. Serve either plain or between buns dipped in the butter. In Louisville, we like to put a generous amount of Henry Bane Sauce on our meat. This sauce was named for one of the early major-domos of the well-known Pendennis Club. Here is the version which an old club member insists was written down for him by Henry Bane *in person.*

Henry Bane Sauce:

1 cup tomato catsup
2 bottles (2 pounds 2 ounces each) Major Grey's East India chutney
2 cups chili sauce
½ cup Worcestershire sauce
6 tablespoons Crosse and Blackwell walnut catsup or sauce
2 teaspoons English or dry mustard
2 to 3 tablespoons Tabasco

I whip all ingredients in a blender to a consistency of thick catsup. But you can grind large pieces of chutney and mix with other ingredients. The original version was too hot for me. I reduced the amount of Tabasco to 1 tablespoon. Start with this and add more if you like a fiery sauce. Bottle and keep on hand to serve with meats and fish.

Deep-South Barbecue for Buns (8 servings)

This barbecue freezes remarkably well and can be reheated without thawing. (For better freezing, omit salt until ready to serve.) Try this for a back-porch buffet supper on a hot day. This list is long, but the cooking is easy.

¼ cup bacon drippings, butter, or margarine
2 tablespoons olive oil (no substitutes)
3 large onions, peeled and diced
2 garlic cloves, crushed
1 pound lean beef, diced
1 pound lean pork, diced
1 pound lean veal, diced
1 tablespoon salt
1 slice hot red pepper or cayenne to taste
Black pepper
1 can (1¼ cups) consommé or stock
2 cans (10½-ounce) tomato purée
2 tablespoons cider vinegar
1 tablespoon molasses or dark brown sugar
½ teaspoon chili powder
⅛ teaspoon ginger
1 tablespoon Worcestershire sauce
Juice of ½ lemon
1 teaspoon sugar
1 teaspoon soy sauce
1 bay leaf
½ teaspoon paprika
⅛ teaspoon cloves
⅛ teaspoon powdered cardamom (optional)
⅛ teaspoon orégano
⅛ teaspoon thyme
¼ cup minced parsley
¼ teaspoon M.S.G.
¼ teaspoon dry mustard

Melt fat in Dutch oven or deep kettle. Add onions and garlic; sauté until yellow. Mix in meat, salt and pepper, and cook until meat no longer seems raw, but do not brown. Stir occasionally. Add other ingredients, bring to a boil, reduce heat, cover, and simmer until mixture cooks to a thick sauce with meat bits, 2 to 4 hours. Stir to keep from sticking. Serve on buns which have been split, buttered, and toasted on the split side only.

Note: Barbecue can be placed between split buns the morning of the party. Wrap each in foil. Just before serving, place in 325° F. oven for 15 minutes. Serve in foil.

Hungarian Lamb Roast with Sour Cream Gravy (6 to 8 servings)

6- to 8-pound leg of lamb
2 cups water
1 cup red wine
1 cup cider vinegar
2 onions, peeled and sliced
1-inch piece ginger root or 1 teaspoon powdered
Grating of nutmeg
1 bay leaf
6 cloves
2 allspice berries
6 crushed peppercorns or ¼ teaspoon pepper
1 blade mace
Juice and rind of ½ lemon
2 tablespoons olive oil or butter
2 cloves garlic

For the lamb, mix together all but the oil or butter and garlic. Marinate lamb at least 12 hours, overnight is better. Turn often, both sides should be well permeated. To cook, remove to baking pan, brown in oil or butter along with garlic cloves. Pour in marinade, cover, and roast in a 350° F. oven until tender—3 to 4 hours. Turn occasionally. Do not let liquid cook away; add more wine and water in equal amounts if needed. Strain and skim the broth.

Sour Cream Gravy

1½ to 2 cups broth
1½ cups sour cream
¼ cup flour
Salt and pepper
Paprika

To the broth, add sour cream mixed with flour, and season with salt and pepper. Pour into top of double boiler. Cook over low heat until consistency of thick cream, stirring constantly.

To serve, slice lamb thin, top each portion with gravy, and dust with paprika.

Old-Time Southern Barbecued Pork (15 servings)

10- to 12-pound shoulder or leg of fresh pork
2 cloves garlic, minced
1 teaspoon seasoning salt
¼ teaspoon chili powder
¼ teaspoon M.S.G.
¼ teaspoon dry mustard
¼ teaspoon garlic salt or powder
2 teaspoons salt or more
¼ teaspoon paprika
¼ teaspoon black pepper
2 tablespoons water
1 onion

Wipe pork. Put all remaining ingredients except water and onion in a bowl and pound until blended. Mix to a paste with water and spread over meat. (This can be done the day before cooking.) Place pork, fat side up, in uncovered pan in a moderate oven, 350° F. Roast 2 to 3 hours until both sides brown; turn every hour. Put unpeeled onion in a separate pan and bake until dark brown and soft. Pour off excess grease. Mash charred onion into juices in roaster.

Barbecue Sauce:

2 teaspoons salt
¼ cup cider vinegar
1 cup tomato purée or sauce
¼ teaspoon allspice
¼ teaspoon nutmeg
1 cup ginger ale or beer
¾ cup chili sauce
¼ teaspoon cloves
¼ teaspoon mace
2 teaspoons Tabasco or 1 teaspoon red pepper (optional)
2 tablespoons dark brown sugar

Combine all ingredients except brown sugar. Pour over pork and return roast to oven. Cover and cook until tender, turning roast on bottom side for an hour or so, then on fat side again. Two more hours should cook a shoulder—a leg will take longer. Add more water if sauce cooks low. I often pour it into another pan when it thickens, add water to the roast, and continue the cooking. When meat is done, mix this liquid with Barbecue Sauce. Serve sauce as is or strain. Thicken with flour-and-water paste if too thin. Just before serving, sprinkle pork with brown sugar; glaze under broiler.

Pork Tenderloins, Farcée (8 to 10 servings)

This fine, winter main dish, served with candied sweet potatoes, a winter fruit salad, hot biscuits, and individual mincemeat pies (well laced with brandy) makes a traditional Southern menu.

2 (2¼ to 2½ pounds) pork tenderloins
Salt and black pepper
Seasoning salt
Flour
4 tablespoons fat
3 cups water
4 tablespoons Worcestershire sauce
2 teaspoons Kitchen Bouquet
½ teaspoon soy sauce
¼ teaspoon M.S.G.
1 bay leaf
2 onions

Split tenderloins down center, but do not cut through. Open out, season, and spread each with half the dressing (recipe below). Secure with skewers or picks. Roll each tenderloin in flour and brown all over in melted fat. Transfer to roaster or large casserole. Pour water over brown crumbs, add other ingredients except onions, bring to a boil, and pour over meat. Cover and bake in a 375° F. oven 1½ to 2 hours, or until tender. Char unpeeled onions in separate pan. Mash into liquid in roaster, cooking at least 10 minutes to give body. Strain 2 cups gravy before serving and thicken with 2 tablespoons flour.

Dressing

2 tablespoons butter, bacon fat, or olive oil
2 onions, peeled and minced
4 stalks celery, diced
Salt and black pepper
6 slices white bread
2 cups milk or consommé
4 eggs
2 tablespoons minced parsley
⅛ teaspoon nutmeg
⅛ teaspoon ginger
¼ teaspoon crumbled sage or thyme

Melt fat, cook onions and celery until soft, about 5 minutes, stirring occasionally. Add salt and pepper, then set aside. Tear bread into small pieces, mix with milk or consommé to a mush, using fingers. Add eggs and beat with a spoon. Then combine with remaining ingredients and add to sautéed vegetables. Cook over low heat, stirring, until mixture leaves sides of pan. It should not cook dry, but hold together and spread without running.

To serve pork tenderloins, remove skewers or picks, and slice.

Ham Baked in Ginger Ale (12 to 20 servings)

12- to 16-pound tenderized ham
1 quart ginger ale or champagne
1 quart water
1 pint Grandma's brand molasses
Whole cloves
Powdered cloves
2 or 3 tablespoons prepared mustard
1 cup dark brown sugar

Wipe ham with damp cloth, place in roaster. Pour over ginger ale or champagne, water, and molasses. Cover and bake in a moderate oven, 350° F., 15 minutes per pound. If liquid evaporates, add more water. Turn ham every hour using spoons to avoid piercing it. When tender, remove from pan, cut fat into diamonds (but not through to meat), stick with cloves, sprinkle powdered cloves over, and spread with mustard and brown sugar. Place ham in a *cold* broiler, then turn on heat and cook until sugar melts and bubbles. (Prepare a day ahead if desired, but do not glaze until near serving time.) Serve hot or cold with one of these sauces.

Jelly Sauce:

Combine a 7-ounce jar tart jelly such as plum, raspberry, or currant, with 1 teaspoon French mustard. Bring to boiling, then serve.

Pineapple-Cider-Raisin Sauce for Ham:

Combine ½ cup each, pineapple juice and cider, 2 tablespoons melted butter, salt and 1 tablespoon flour mixed first with a little juice. Bring to boiling. Add 1 tablespoon prepared horseradish, ¼ cup raisins, and 1 teaspoon brown sugar. Let boil, then serve.

Versailles Ham Loaf with Chutney Sauce (8 servings)

Here's another of Jesse Bond Bolton's fine recipes. It is an excellent way to turn leftover baked ham into a real party dish.

Loaf:

1½ pounds (3 cups) ground baked ham, fat removed
1½ pounds fresh pork, ground
2 eggs, beaten
½ cup freshly-made bread or cracker crumbs
1 cup milk
Salt and pepper

Topping:

½ cup brown sugar
1½ tablespoons dry mustard

Chutney Sauce

8-ounce jar currant jelly (1 cup)
¼ cup sherry
1 cup Major Grey's chutney
1 teaspoon Worcestershire sauce

Mix the loaf ingredients together. Place in a well-greased oblong baking dish. Spread on topping. Set oven at 400° F. and brown the loaf. Reduce heat to 350° and bake until meat is done, 2 to 2½ hours. Heat sauce ingredients until blended and bubbling, stir continually to keep from sticking. Transfer ham loaf to platter. Serve sauce separately

Veal Scaloppine with Marsala-Olive Sauce

This gourmet specialty can be prepared beforehand, reheated, and placed on a food warmer or in a chafing dish at the table.

8 veal birds or thin pieces from leg, about 3 pounds
Salt and black pepper
1 cup flour (about)
½ cup olive oil (no substitutes)
1 pound mushrooms
1 clove garlic, sliced (optional)
¾ cup Italian tomato paste
3 cans (2¼ cups) consommé or water
1 bay leaf
¼ teaspoon basil
¼ teaspoon rosemary
1 cup Marsala or sherry
½ cup green olives, seeds removed
1 lemon, sliced thin
Minced parsley

The veal should be only ¼ inch thick; each piece large enough for a serving. Sprinkle with salt and pepper, dip each side in flour, place between pieces of waxed paper, then pound thin with a wooden mallet. Remove paper—don't worry if veal tears a bit. Brown in olive oil. Take from pan with a pancake turner. Sauté fresh mushrooms, caps and stems separated, and garlic if using, 5 minutes. Stir occasionally. Mix in tomato paste, consommé or water, bay leaf, and herbs. Place veal in sauce. Cover, turn heat very low, and simmer until tender—25 to 30 minutes. Correct seasonings, add Marsala or sherry, and olives. Heat and serve, garnishing with lemon slices dipped in parsley.

Veal Bourguignonne (8 servings)

This inexpensive main dish is one of the most delightful of all French stews. We usually serve ours with boiled noodles topped with crisp, crushed, raw noodles browned in butter.

3 pounds lean veal, cut in 1½-inch pieces
1 onion, peeled and sliced thin
1 carrot, scraped and sliced thin
1 clove garlic, crushed
2 cups red wine
4 tablespoons brandy
1 bay leaf
¼ teaspoon thyme
¼ teaspoon rosemary
¼ teaspoon black pepper
*¼ teaspoon cloves or Kitchen Spice **

Marinate veal in above ingredients for 24 hours or overnight. Drain meat and reserve marinade.

¼ cup butter (about)
1 pound mushrooms, quartered
6 shallots, minced
4 onions, peeled and sliced
4 carrots, scraped and sliced
2 cloves garlic, sliced thin
1 tablespoon salt
1 teaspoon sugar
1 tablespoon Worcestershire sauce
1 teaspoon soy sauce
1½ cups bouillon or consommé
¼ cup flour (about)

Melt butter or margarine. Brown marinated veal, stirring occasionally; remove to a large casserole. Sauté vegetables, using more fat if needed. Then place in casserole with other ingredients except flour. Pour in marinade. Cover and cook in a 350° F. oven for 2½ to 3 hours. Veal should be tender enough to cut with a fork. (If liquid cooks too low, add equal amounts of consommé or bouillon and red wine. There should be about 3 cups left when meat is done.) Thicken broth with a flour-and-water paste and allow to cook until meat and vegetables are coated. Make this stew beforehand if you wish, reheat, then thicken just before serving.

Pickled Tongue in Mushroom-Wine Sauce (6 servings)

2- to 2½-pound pickled beef tongue
3 stalks celery with leaves or 1 bunch celery tops
3 onions, peeled and sliced thin
3 sprigs parsley
¼ teaspoon thyme
1 bay leaf
2 teaspoons salt
¼ teaspoon black pepper

¼ cup butter, margarine or olive oil
½ pound fresh mushrooms, quartered
2 or 3 tablespoons flour
2 cups stock, strained
1 tablespoon Worcestershire sauce
¼ teaspoon seasoning salt
¼ teaspoon soy sauce
4 or 5 tablespoons white wine
3 tablespoons minced parsley
½ teaspoon sugar, if needed

Cook pickled or smoked tongue in a pressure cooker with 1 quart water and all ingredients in the left column, 1 to 1½ hours at 15 pounds' pressure. Or use a large kettle with 2 to 3 quarts water for 3 to 6 hours depending on the age of the tongue. When tender, remove skin, cut tongue into ½-inch-thick slices. Prepare the sauce.

Melt fat in skillet. Sauté mushrooms over low heat, covered, about 5 minutes. Stir occasionally. Add flour, mix to a paste, then slowly add stock, stirring until thickened. Add other ingredients. Prepare sauce ahead if desired. Let tongue slices simmer 15 minutes in sauce before serving.

Sweetbread Hash (8 servings)

Chicken hash is good but how about making it with sweetbreads for a change? They're fine for that cocktail-supper when you want something simple, yet special. This is a versatile recipe; make the hash ahead, chill, and reheat at serving time, or freeze the prepared dish.

4 large or 8 medium sweetbreads boiled and cut in 1-inch cubes
½ cup melted butter or olive oil
1 green pepper, minced
½ cup minced celery
4 large onions, peeled and diced
¼ cup flour
2 cups sweetbread stock
1 cup cream or evaporated milk
4 teaspoons Worcestershire sauce
1 teaspoon Kitchen Bouquet or Browning *
½ teaspoon soy sauce
¼ teaspoon seasoning salt
¼ teaspoon Kitchen Spice *
Salt and black pepper
¼ teaspoon M.S.G.
¼ cup minced parsley
Paprika

For the sweetbreads, prepare this rich sauce. Heat fat in skillet. Sauté green pepper, celery, and onions for 4 or 5 minutes or until vegetables are yellow but not browned. Add flour, stir to a paste, then pour in sweetbread stock. When smooth, add cream or milk and other ingredients except paprika. Correct seasonings. Mixture should be consistency of a medium cream sauce. Add sweetbreads, heat thoroughly. Pour into a serving dish, sprinkle with paprika and take to the table. Spoon hash over rice, toast points, or into patty shells.

Note: See Sweetbread Vichyssoise for directions for preparing sweetbreads.

Variations: Add ½ cup sherry and 2 diced pimientos just before serving. And stretch hash if you wish with a couple of sliced hard-cooked eggs.

Fold 2 cups mixed frozen green peas and carrots (cooked and drained) into the sweetbread-and-sherry mixture, just before sending to the table. This makes an especially nice all-in-one dish with 3 more servings.

Or add ½ pound of slivered mushrooms. Sauté with other vegetables when you make the basic hash recipe.

Pride-of-the-Bluegrass Mustard (8 servings)

Here's one of the best meat sauces ever to come out of a Kentucky kitchen. Serve it with smoked tongue, corned beef, wieners, or baked ham. If any is left, store in a jar with a tight lid and keep refrigerated.

2 tablespoons dry mustard
1½ tablespoons flour
½ teaspoon salt
3 tablespoons sugar
5 tablespoons cider vinegar
9 tablespoons beer or water
2 tablespoons melted butter

Whip all ingredients smooth in a blender. Or make a paste of dry ingredients with vinegar and add beer or water slowly. (Stale beer can be used.) Stir in butter. Pour mixture into double boiler and beat with a wooden spoon until the consistency of a thick cream sauce. It takes about 4 minutes of constant beating. Serve hot or cold.

15 GARDEN TRUCK

During the early nineteenth century, the first fresh green peas to reach London in early spring sold for a guinea a pound. Truck gardening was a profitable business then, respectable too, judging by the titled men and women who made many an honest pound by the sweat of their gardeners' brows. In spite of their appreciation of good food, however, even wealth could not bring to Georgian housewives, green beans and tomatoes in February, mushrooms in July, or asparagus in December. Each season had but brief offerings of fresh produce, and it took real effort to dry, salt, pickle, or preserve garden favorites so as to vary the monotony of common root vegetables—the only ones which could survive unspoiled through the winter months.

Today, due to the miracle of modern transportation and the genius of Mr. Clarence Birdseye, we can have any vegetables we wish and at any time of year. With a wide selection always at hand, we should serve vegetables often, for they are inexpensive, tasty, and easy to prepare, and they bring variety and interest to our modern cocktail-suppers. Here are recipes which can be prepared *beforehand* and reheated without damage to flavor or texture.

A TOUCH OF GREEN

Asparagus in Sesame-Seed Butter (6 servings)

Brown 1 cup butter in a skillet; mix in ½ cup sesame seeds and stir until parched a pale caramel color. Quickly add juice of 1 lemon and pour over 2 pounds fresh cooked asparagus, drained, or 2 (10-ounce) packages frozen asparagus, cooked and drained.

Note: Green Peas in Sesame-Seed Butter can be prepared the same way. And broccoli is good with this sauce, too.

Green Asparagus, Vinaigrette (See recipe.)

Green Beans and Eggplant, Hartnett (8 servings)

This is a creation of Marge Hartnett and her gifted cook, Anna. They were good enough to share this recipe. It is one of the finest cocktail-supper vegetable dishes.

8 thin slices eggplant, pared
Flour
Butter
3 (10-ounce) packages frozen Frenched green beans
2 cups Well-seasoned Cream Sauce (See recipe)
½ cup slivered or ground almonds
½ cup butter

Sauté floured eggplant slices in butter. Place on serving platter. Cook and drain beans; mix with cream sauce, and top each slice of eggplant with a mound of beans. Brown the almonds in ½ cup butter and dribble a good tablespoon over each serving.

Brussels Sprouts, de Luxe (8 servings)

Boil 2 pounds Brussels sprouts in salted water 10 to 20 minutes or until tender. Drain and combine with 2 cups Well-seasoned Cream Sauce (see recipe). Pour over sprouts ½ cup pecans sautéed in ½ cup butter or margarine.

Note: Green beans are also delicious in this sauce. Vary by using almonds or peanuts.

Red Cabbage, Sweet-and-Sour (8 servings)

¼ cup bacon drippings or butter
1 large onion, peeled and minced
2 tablespoons flour
1 large firm head red cabbage, shredded fine
1 bay leaf
Salt and black pepper
2 whole cloves
2 apples, pared and shredded
⅓ cup cider vinegar or more
⅓ cup dark brown sugar or more

Melt fat, add onion and flour, stir until brown. Pour in 1 cup water, stirring to make a smooth sauce. Add cabbage, enough water to barely cover, bay leaf, salt, and pepper. Cover, bring to a hard boil. Reduce heat and simmer 30 to 40 minutes. Add rest of ingredients; cook ½ hour longer. Cabbage should be tender by then and sauce spicy. Correct flavoring to your taste. Serve with Hungarian Lamb or any other roast.

Sauerkraut in Wine with Caraway Seeds (6 to 8 servings)

2 pounds sauerkraut
1 quart stock or water
4 tablespoons dark brown sugar
1 large onion, peeled and minced
⅔ cup white wine
1 teaspoon caraway seeds
1 apple, pared and shredded
Salt and cayenne

Put all ingredients in a Dutch oven or deep kettle. Cover, let come to a hard boil, then reduce heat to a simmer. Cook 1½ to 2 hours until thoroughly blended and kraut is tender. Prepare a day ahead, refrigerate, and reheat before serving if you wish.

Cream O' Corn (8 servings)

Put 8 tender ears of corn, prepared for cooking, in a large kettle of boiling water. Cover and cook 3 minutes. Drain and cool, then wrap corn in waxed paper or foil, and refrigerate. This can be done the day before. Split each grain with a corn creamer or sharp knife. Hold ears over bowl and using a dull knife, scrape out kernels. Melt ⅓ cup butter in a skillet, add corn, 1 tablespoon sugar, salt, and freshly-ground pepper. Heat thoroughly, stirring constantly. This simple recipe is one of the best ways to serve corn at a cocktail-supper.

Alabama Succotash (8 servings)

An excellent summer vegetable combination.

1 quart young Lima beans
¼ teaspoon black pepper
2 teaspoons sugar
2 teaspoons salt
1 quart water
6 ears corn
¼ cup butter
6 tablespoons cream or evaporated milk

Cook Lima beans with pepper, sugar, and salt in water, covered, for 25 to 30 minutes, or until tender. Have heat high at first, then lower to a simmer. Add corn cut from the cob. If desired, split grains with a corn creamer or knife and press out kernels. Simmer for another 10 to 15 minutes or until corn is done. Add butter and cream or milk and stir until mixture thickens. Correct seasonings and serve.

Green Peas, Chinese Style (6 servings)

2 (10-ounce) packages frozen peas
2 medium onions, peeled and diced
1 cup diced celery
½ cup olive or salad oil
2 teaspoons cornstarch
2 cups chicken stock or use 4 chicken bouillon cubes
½ teaspoon M.S.G.
¼ teaspoon soy sauce
Salt to taste

Place vegetables in a large skillet with hot oil. (Use part olive oil if possible.) Have flame high and when peas are sputtering, cover, turn heat low and sauté 10 to 15 minutes. Stir occasionally. If vegetables are not done, cook 5 more minutes, but it's Chinese style to have them crisp. Mix cornstarch with ¼ cup stock, then add rest. Combine with vegetables and cook until slightly thickened and transparent. Add seasonings. Cook 1 minute longer and serve. This can be prepared ahead and reheated.

Water Chestnuts and Peas in Bouillon (6 to 8 servings)

Follow recipe for Green Peas, Chinese Style, substituting 3 cups beef bouillon for chicken stock. Sliver 16 Chinese canned water chestnuts and sauté with other vegetables.

Minted Peas (6 servings)

Cook 2 (10-ounce) packages frozen peas. Just before serving, add 2 tablespoons minted vinegar (see recipe for Herb Vinegar) and ¼ cup melted butter.

Spinach and Mushrooms (4 or 5 servings)

12-ounce package chopped, frozen spinach
4 thin strips bacon
4 tablespoons bacon fat
1 small onion, peeled and chopped
½ pound fresh mushrooms or 3-ounce can broiled mushrooms
2 tablespoons flour
Salt and black pepper
1 cup milk
1 teaspoon Worcestershire sauce
¼ teaspoon soy or Maggi sauce
⅛ teaspoon M.S.G.

Cook spinach according to directions on package. Drain and put aside. Meanwhile fry bacon, then drain on absorbent paper, and crumble. Sauté onion and slivered mushrooms in bacon fat 5 minutes, stirring constantly. Add flour and stir till golden. Add salt and pepper and slowly mix in milk. Add other seasonings and spinach; stir until thickened to a purée. Pour into a serving dish and sprinkle with bacon.

Spinach à la Russe (6 servings)

Mix 2 (12-ounce) packages chopped, frozen spinach, cooked according to directions on the package and drained, with Cossack's Delight (see recipe page 74). Really a superb dish!

Cinnamon-baked Acorn Squash (Allow ½ squash per serving)

Cut squash in half, remove seeds. Boil in lightly-salted water for 15 minutes. Drain well. Put in a well-greased baking dish, cut side up. In each half spread mixture of: 1 heaping teaspoon dark brown sugar, 1 teaspoon softened butter, dash of cinnamon, and grating of nutmeg. This can be prepared well ahead. Thirty minutes before serving, bake squash in a hot oven, 450° F. until tender and sugar is glazed. (Reduce to 350° if sugar gets too dark.) Baste several times. Serve with pork or ham. The squash will remain hot on a food warmer for a long time.

Stuffed Acorn Squash (Allow ½ a squash per serving)

Boil squash as above. Fill with Dressing (See recipe for Pork Tenderloins, Farcée). Sprinkle with plain bread crumbs or with part grated Cheddar or Parmesan cheese. Bake in hot oven, 450° F., until crumbs brown. Reduce heat to 350° and bake about 40 minutes. These squash are nice to serve with fowl when the birds themselves have not been stuffed.

Savory Stuffed Cymlings (6 servings)

David Minefield, Marion Green's ingenious cook, concocted this heavenly dish to serve with salmon mousse. Stuff squash the day before the party and give the final baking just before serving. They stand well on a hot plate at the buffet table.

6 cymlings (scalloped summer squash) of uniform size, 3 or 4 inches in diameter
1 large onion, peeled and minced
½ cup butter or margarine
¼ teaspoon curry powder
Salt and pepper
*¼ teaspoon Sensation Seasoner **
1 teaspoon sugar
2 beef bouillon cubes or 1 teaspoon B.V. paste
4 or 5 tablespoons cracker crumbs or more
½ cup milk
Extra crumbs
6 tablespoons butter

Boil cymlings in salted water 10 minutes, drain and cover with cold water. When cool enough to handle, wipe dry, and cut a thin slice from the top of each unpeeled squash. Cut out as much pulp as possible leaving a ¼-inch-thick shell. Chop pulp fine, cook 5 minutes over low heat in water barely to cover. Drain well and mash. Cook onion in melted fat with seasonings and sugar until onion is soft and yellow—about 5 minutes. Mash in bouillon cubes or B.V. paste and dissolve. Add crumbs and mix well. Pour in milk and cook until sauce thickens. (If not thick enough, add more crumbs.) Combine with cooked pulp.

Stuff shells and place side by side in a lightly-greased baking dish about quarter full of water. Sprinkle with bread crumbs and dot each squash with butter. Bake in a 375° F. oven until tops brown and squash seem done—about 45 minutes. Serve hot in the baking dish. If preparing stuffed squash ahead, add extra crumbs and butter before baking.

Baked Zucchini, Siena (8 servings)

Prepare this for baking the morning of the party.

8 zucchini, 4 or 5 inches long, cut in 1/4-inch slices
4 medium onions, peeled and sliced thin
2 cloves garlic, slivered
1 green pepper, minced
1/4 teaspoon thyme
1/4 teaspoon basil
1/4 cup olive oil
1/4 cup butter or margarine
1/4 teaspoon soy sauce
1 teaspoon Worcestershire sauce
Salt, pepper, seasoning salt
1 teaspoon sugar or more
4 tomatoes, peeled and sliced thin
1 cup grated Parmesan, Swiss, or Cheddar cheese
1/2 cup freshly-made butter cracker crumbs

Simmer zucchini (unpeeled if tender) with onions, garlic, green pepper, and herbs in heated fat. Cook covered 10 minutes, stirring occasionally. Add soy and Worcestershire sauce, seasonings, and sugar. In a 2-quart lightly-buttered casserole, place a layer of tomatoes, a layer of zucchini, then tomatoes, until all have been used. When ready to bake, sprinkle with cheese, top with crumbs. Bake in a 350° F. oven until browned and cheese is bubbly, about 40 to 45 minutes. Serve hot.

FILLED WITH SATISFACTION

Barley (6 servings)

Put 1 cup pearl barley in 4 cups chicken broth with a sliced clove garlic, 2 stalks celery, sliced, and a peeled, minced onion. Cook in a 6-quart pressure cooker 40 minutes at 15 pounds' pressure. Or simmer in a deep kettle, covered, with 6 cups broth (and water) for 1 1/2 to 2 hours. Add more water if needed. Serve instead of rice. This is particularly good with goose, wild duck, or quail.

Note: Add chopped giblets, neck, and wings for flavor.

Chestnut Whip (8 servings)

Serve this instead of whipped potatoes. It holds up much better on the warming tray, and goes very well with poultry and game.

4 cups peeled chestnuts (see page 137)
2 cans (2½ cups) beef bouillon
¼ cup butter
1 cup heavy cream
Salt and cayenne pepper

Cook chestnuts in bouillon, covered, until very tender—about 20 to 25 minutes. By that time most of the bouillon will have evaporated. If not, drain chestnuts, and reserve liquid. Put chestnuts through a food mill or ricer, then beat with an electric mixer if handy. Add butter while still hot enough to melt it. (Otherwise melt butter first.) Fold in whipped cream and season. If mixture is dry, add a little of the bouillon. It should be light and fluffy.

Southern Grits Bread (6 servings)

This is an alternate for the more common spoon bread. It is a fine addition to cocktail-suppers when a roast is the main dish.

2 cups milk
½ cup grits
1 teaspoon butter or margarine
½ teaspoon salt
1 egg

Pour boiling milk over grits; stir to keep from lumping. Cook until thick, stirring constantly. Add butter or margarine; mix until it melts, then add salt and well-beaten egg. This can be made ahead, poured into a well-greased 9-inch baking dish or skillet, and refrigerated until baking time. Bake in a 400° F. oven until bread rises and top browns. It will look something like corn bread. Cut into wedges and serve.

Big Hominy Chili Casserole (8 to 10 servings)

I had this distinctive dish at the Bond family home one brisk winter day. It accompanied a Kentucky country ham —a memorable meal indeed.

2 tablespoons butter
1 tablespoon cornstarch
1 cup cream or top milk
1 tablespoon Worcestershire sauce
5 drops Tabasco or dash cayenne
2 teaspoons red chili powder or more
Salt and pepper to taste
8½-ounce can ripe olives and liquor
2 No. 2½ cans big hominy, drained
½ pound aged Cheddar cheese, shredded or grated

Add melted butter and cornstarch to milk. Beat well or whip in a blender. Cook in top of double boiler until thick, stirring constantly. Add seasonings, sliced olives (seeds removed) and liquor; cook and blend well, still stirring. Remove from heat and mix in hominy. Correct seasoning. (There should be enough chili powder to color mixture a definite red.) Pour into a lightly-greased 2½-quart casserole. Do this the day before if you like. Place casserole in a 375° F. oven 30 to 40 minutes or until sauce is bubbly. Then sprinkle with cheese, brown under grill, and serve at once. This will remain hot a long time on a warming tray.

Cheese-Noodle Ring (6 to 8 servings)

3 cups boiled drained noodles
4 eggs, separated
1½ cups milk
1¼ cups grated Swiss, Gruyère, or Cheddar cheese
1 tablespoon Worcestershire sauce
1 tablespoon catsup
Salt and black pepper

Place noodles in a bowl. Slowly add egg yolks and milk, then cheese, seasonings, and last of all, well-beaten whites. Spoon into a buttered ring mold and place in pan a quarter full of water. Bake in a 375° F. oven 30 to 40 minutes or until firm. Loosen edges and turn out onto a round platter.

Bahamian Peas and Rice (6 servings)

This native Bahamian dish was given me by a resident of Bimini. Each cook prepares it in an individual way, but the results are similar. You can make it ahead.

1 cup dried pigeon peas or lentils
Salt and hot red pepper to taste
4 slices bacon
2 large onions, peeled and diced
1 large tomato, peeled, sliced, and seeds removed
1 cup rice
3 cups meat stock or use *3 bouillon cubes*

Soak peas or lentils overnight in water. Drain. Put in a saucepan with fresh water to cover. Bring to a boil, add salt and hot pepper. Cover, lower heat, and simmer until tender. Add more water and seasoning if necessary. Or cook in a pressure cooker with 2 cups water, ½ teaspoon salt, ⅛ teaspoon cayenne or 1 tiny red pepper pod for 15 minutes at 15 pounds' pressure. If not tender, cook a little longer. Fry bacon, drain, and set aside. Sauté onions in bacon fat until soft but not brown. Add tomato, rice, and stock. Cover, and as soon as mixture boils lower heat. Simmer until rice is cooked, stirring occasionally. It should be moist. Fold in drained peas or lentils, correct seasoning. When ready to serve, crumble bacon over top.

Triple Cheese-stuffed Potatoes (12 servings)

Do all but the final baking a day ahead for convenience.

8 large baking potatoes
½ cup melted butter or margarine
Salt and black pepper
3 or 4 tablespoons milk
¾ cup shredded or grated Cheddar cheese
1 cup shredded or grated Swiss cheese
1 cup thick cream sauce
½ teaspoon Kitchen Bouquet
4 tablespoons heavy cream
1 teaspoon Worcestershire sauce
12 tablespoons grated Parmesan cheese

Choose potatoes of the same size. Scrub and dry them. Bake in a moderate oven, 350° F., 1 to 2 hours or until done. Split in half lengthwise (according to the way they lie evenly to avoid tipping when stuffed). Remove center, leaving shells intact, and put through a ricer or food mill. While very hot, add butter or margarine, salt, pepper, and enough milk to make a moist purée. Beat in Cheddar cheese. This should be enough filling for 12 potato shells.

Pile filling into shells just to the top. Level with back of spoon, make a canal the length of the potato, pressing shell so two ridges form. Mix together everything except the Parmesan cheese. Cook in top of double boiler. Stir until cheese melts and mixture is very thick. Pour sauce into "canals" and smooth well. If prepared the day ahead, wrap and refrigerate. Just before reheating, sprinkle a tablespoon of Parmesan over each half. Heat in a 350° F. oven, then transfer to grill and leave until brown. The centers will puff like a soufflé. Serve at once.

Rice Ring (6 servings)

Boil 1 cup rice in salted water 20 minutes or until done. Drain. Pack into a greased ring mold. Place in pan quarter full of hot water and bake 1 hour in a 350° F. oven. Unmold and fill center. This ring is especially good for meat or sea food in highly-seasoned sauces.

Rice and Cheese Ring (6 servings)

Substitute 3 cups boiled, drained rice for noodles in Cheese-Noodle Ring (see recipe page 176).

Parsley Rice (6 servings)

To 3 cups boiled, drained, fluffy rice add salt and freshly-ground pepper to taste. Fold in ⅓ cup melted butter or margarine and ¼ cup finely-minced parsley. Dust with paprika.

Saffron Rice (See recipe.)

Chinese Fried Rice (6 servings)

3 tablespoons butter or salad oil
2 tablespoons olive oil
½ cup diced celery
1 medium onion, peeled and diced
1 green pepper, diced
2 cups cooked drained rice
½ teaspoon soy sauce
¼ teaspoon M.S.G.
Salt and pepper
Garlic or seasoning salt

Melt fat in a deep skillet. Cook vegetables until soft, about 5 minutes. Stir constantly. Add rice and seasonings. Serve as soon as rice is hot. This can be prepared ahead with just reheating left till party time. This rice also keeps well on the warming plate.

New Orleans Rice Bread (6 servings)

This old-time recipe comes from Mina Chambers' mother, and the directions from her houseman, George Hughes. Serve it for your hot dish when cold ham, turkey, or other cold cuts are on the menu. Round out your meal with buttered, toasted French bread, French endive and lettuce salad, Brie or Camembert cheese with toasted water biscuits, and hot coffee.

It can be made a day ahead and refrigerated, but rises a little higher if the egg whites and baking powder are added just before baking.

1 cup water-ground white corn meal
2 cups boiling water
1 teaspoon salt or more
2 tablespoons bacon drippings, butter, or vegetable shortening
1 cup milk
2 eggs, separated
1 cup fluffy cooked rice
3 teaspoons baking powder

Slowly pour corn meal into a saucepan with the boiling water, stirring constantly. Stir until mixture makes a thick mush, free from lumps. Add salt and fat and remove from stove. Slowly beat in milk, making a smooth batter. Add egg yolks and beat again. Mix in rice. Set aside to cool to room temperature or refrigerate. When cooled, fold in well-beaten egg whites and baking powder, or wait until just ready to bake. Pour into a buttered, 2-quart baking dish and set in a fairly hot oven, 400° F., about 35 to 45 minutes, or until top and sides are a delightful brown and the bread has risen and seems light. Serve at once. When placed on a hot plate throughout the meal, the bread may fall a little, but its lightness and flavor will not be affected.

Hogdenville Hot Pot (8 servings)

In 1954, when the Women's Club of Hogdenville, Kentucky, entertained President Eisenhower at a luncheon, he seemed especially pleased with this regional casserole dish. Camille Glen has given me her recipe for it.

1 cup fresh cracker crumbs
2 cups Well-seasoned Cream Sauce (see recipe below)
2 cups shredded Cheddar cheese
4 canned pimientos, diced
4 hard-cooked eggs, sliced
3 tablespoons butter

In a well-buttered 2-quart casserole, place a thin layer of crumbs, cover with a thin layer of cream sauce, top with a layer of cheese, a sprinkling of pimientos, then eggs. Continue until ingredients are used up; be sure crumbs are on top. If you wish, mix ¼ cup crumbs and ¼ cup cheese for top. This can be made ahead and refrigerated.

When ready to cook, dot with butter. Bake in a 350° F. oven 30 to 40 minutes or until bubbling and top is brown. Do not cook too stiff; it should be a little runny. This keeps hot on a warmer throughout the meal.

Well-seasoned Cream Sauce:

1 cup milk
1 cup cream
¼ cup melted butter or margarine
¼ cup flour
1 teaspoon Worcestershire sauce
¼ teaspoon Kitchen Bouquet
½ teaspoon salt or more
Dash Tabasco or cayenne pepper

Whip all ingredients in a blender, then cook in top of a double boiler until thick, stirring constantly. Or use any preferred method.

NICE ASIDES

Old-fashioned Crunchy Cucumber Chips (About 4 pints)

These crisp, sweet pickles make a nice *special* addition to the buffet table.

2 quarts processed large sour pickles (not dills)
1 pint cider vinegar
1 large clove garlic, slivered
1 tablespoon whole cloves
1 tablespoon whole allspice
1 hot red pepper, cut in 3 pieces
1 bay leaf
1 piece stick cinnamon
5 cups sugar (all white, or half dark brown, packed)
1 tablespoon celery seed
1 tablespoon mustard seed
1 tablespoon black peppercorns (optional)
1 piece dried ginger root
½ cup olive oil

Drain off brine and cut pickles crosswise into ¼-inch slices. Place in a half-gallon jar or crock with a tight-fitting lid. Mix all remaining ingredients except olive oil, and bring to a boil; then cool. Pour over pickles in jar and let stand for 24 hours, turning jar upside down and shaking every now and then. Make sure liquid covers chips. Add oil, and continue shaking and turning jar several times a day for a week.

Drain cucumbers; save liquid. Place the crisp, translucent chips in pint jars. (Fill but do not pack down.) Shake up marinade and pour into jars until chips are covered. Seal and store. These chips will keep indefinitely.

Pickled Green Peppers (6 to 8 servings)

We discovered this treat in Siena and have since served these peppers often as an accompaniment for cold meat.

Select 3 or 4 large green peppers, mature ones that have a thick pulp. To peel (and it is not as hard as it sounds), put peppers under broiler, turn often, till they blister and are brown all over. Put under cold running water and peel. Or bake in a moderate oven, 375° F., 30 to 40 minutes and peel under running water. Once you've tasted peeled peppers you won't want to eat them any other way.

Cut in half, remove core and seeds. Cut into ½-inch strips. Add 1 tablespoon lemon or lime juice, 2 tablespoons red wine vinegar, 3 or 4 tablespoons olive oil, salt, and freshly-ground pepper. Cover and marinate at least 2 hours. These peppers will keep fresh about 2 weeks if refrigerated.

Hawaiian Pineapple Pickle (6 servings)

In Hawaii, where I first tasted this wonderful relish, it was sometimes colored green, sometimes red. But always thoroughly chilled and delicious. My thanks to Patricia Collier of Dole Pineapple for letting me include this recipe.

No. 2 or 2½ can pineapple chunks in heavy sirup
¾ cup cider vinegar
1 to 1¼ cups sugar
6 whole allspice berries
6 whole cloves
6-inch piece stick cinnamon
½ teaspoon powdered coriander seeds (optional)
Few grains salt
Green or red vegetable coloring

Drain pineapple, reserving ¾ cup sirup. Put all ingredients (except pineapple chunks and coloring) in a saucepan and cook 10 minutes. Add drained pineapple, bring to a hard boil. Skim if necessary. Remove from heat, add coloring to your liking. Cool, place in a jar, cover and refrigerate. Do not serve for at least 24 hours—it's even better after several days.

Old-South Brandied Peaches (About 30)

These are the peaches served with roast duck or goose, or with ham in most Southern homes.

8 pounds firm medium-sized peaches (about 30), peeled
6 cups sugar
½ cup water
4 large pieces stick cinnamon
1 teaspoon whole cloves
1 teaspoon whole allspice
1 teaspoon whole or powdered coriander seeds (optional)
2 cups brandy or bourbon whisky

Make a sirup of sugar and water in a large kettle. Add spices and bring to a hard boil. Reduce heat and simmer 5 minutes. Add peaches; do not crowd them. Simmer about 10 to 20 minutes, until tender. Freestone (which I prefer) will take less time than cling. Test with a cake tester or broom straw. Remove to a deep pottery bowl. When all peaches are done, strain sirup over them. In the Old South, the peaches were given a sun bath at this point, with a piece of cheesecloth over the bowl. Do so if you wish. Cool peaches in the sirup, then add brandy or bourbon. Place in jars, pour sirup over them, filling jars. Seal and store. Let peaches age for 3 weeks before serving.

Note: To peel peaches, boil 1 gallon water with ¼ cup Sal or washing soda (not cooking). Put in not more than 6 peaches at a time. Ripe ones require only 1 minute; firm ones 2 to 5 minutes. As soon as peaches darken and fuzz begins to flake off, transfer with a slotted spoon to a deep kettle of cold water. Peel and drop at once into a gallon of water mixed with a scant tablespoon salt and 2 tablespoons vinegar. This will prevent fruit turning dark.

16 SALAD SUMMER-Y

Salads have an ancient history; the very word is derived from the Latin *sal,* meaning salt. In *Cookery and Dining in Imperial Rome* by Apicius, we find this modern salad recipe: "Endives and lettuce (are dressed) with brine, a little oil, and chopped onion; instead of the real lettuce in winter-time, the endives are taken out of the pickle (and are dressed) with honey or vinegar."

In the Middle Ages, the British discovered that "messes of greens" were edible, but left it to the more ingenious Renaissance Italians to make a "cult of the salad" and a "ritual of the dressing." In Queen Elizabeth's time, a good salad graced every fine dinner table, and during the reign of Queen Anne, salad became a serious enough subject for literary treatment. At the end of the seventeenth century, John Evelyn published his *Acetaria, A Discourse of Sallets,* which might still be considered the best essay on the subject. "What is a sallet? . . . A peculiar composition of certain crude and fresh herbs such as are, or may safely be eaten with some acetous juice, oyl, salt, etc., to give them a grateful gust and vehicle." In Evelyn's day many more uncooked greens and vegetables found their way into a salad than we are likely to enjoy today—artichokes and asparagus were eaten raw, roots of the daisy, dock, elder flowers, sorrel, and others. He lists only one salad dressing, but it is an excellent one. You'll find it with Chicken Salmagundi in this chapter.

SIDE-DISH SALADS

Spanish Green Salad

The Spaniards, who love salads, serve either a variety of mixed greens, or a combination of croutons fried in Garlic Oil (see recipe in Salad Make-up), mixed greens, pickled mushrooms, and a few anchovies and sardines with:

Herbed Spanish Dressing (6 servings)

2-ounce can anchovies
¼ teaspoon black pepper
1 small onion, peeled and minced
1 clove garlic, crushed
⅓ cup red wine vinegar or sherry vinegar
⅔ cup olive oil (no substitutes)
1 tablespoon tomato catsup
1 teaspoon Worcestershire sauce
Dash Tabasco or cayenne pepper
¼ teaspoon each: thyme, basil, orégano

Place anchovies and their oil, pepper, onion, and garlic in a wooden bowl or mortar. Mash or grind to a paste. Add other ingredients, and serve as is or press through a food mill. Or whip all ingredients smooth in a blender. This keeps well when bottled. Serve in a separate bowl.

Giacomoni's Vegetable Salad (6 servings)

When we were in Naples last, we had this salad at Giacomoni's excellent restaurant in the heart of town. A large pottery bowl was lined with crisp yellow-green lettuce and these vegetables were on top: baby zucchini, uncooked and unpeeled, in ¼-inch slices, (cook if you prefer); boiled, Italian green beans; cooked artichoke hearts; slivered, cooked carrots; peeled, quartered, fresh tomatoes. All were arranged like spokes of a wheel. The salad was brought to our table and a dressing mixed before our eyes. I watched carefully to see what ingredients were used; I've had to guess at the amounts, however, since none were measured accurately.

Neapolitan Dressing

2 spilling tablespoons mayonnaise
1 tablespoon Worcestershire sauce
1 tablespoon prepared French mustard
3 or 4 tablespoons lime or lemon juice
½ cup olive oil
Salt and black pepper

Beat ingredients together with a fork. Pour over the vegetables and mix with two forks, then serve.

Scandinavian Spiced Beets (6 servings)

2 cups sliced canned beets
½ cup canned beet juice
1 cup cider vinegar
⅓ cup sugar
½ teaspoon salt
½ teaspoon cloves
⅛ teaspoon allspice
¼ teaspoon cinnamon
⅛ teaspoon garlic powder or salt
⅛ teaspoon cardamom (optional)
⅛ teaspoon coriander (optional)

Mix all ingredients and refrigerate in a covered jar until thoroughly chilled. These beets keep for a long time.

Chef's Salad, Louisville (8 servings)

1 bunch water cress (about ¼ pound)
1 small head Bibb or Cos lettuce
1 head iceberg lettuce
2 tomatoes, peeled and quartered
4 stalks celery, diced
8 ripe or green olives
2 teaspoons capers
1 green pepper, diced
2 spring onions, minced
4 hard-cooked eggs, sliced
4 unpeeled radishes, slivered
1 tablespoon minced dill pickle
Salt and black pepper to taste
¾ cup Roquefort or Danish Bleu Dressing or more (see recipe)
½ cup cooked shredded chicken
½ cup cooked shredded ham

Shred salad greens and place in a deep bowl. Add all ingredients except salt and pepper, dressing, chicken, and ham. Cover and refrigerate ahead if desired. At serving time, season, mix with two forks, and add just enough dressing to thoroughly coat ingredients. Sprinkle chicken and ham over top.

Note: To serve 12 add 1 peeled, slivered avocado; a small can drained, miniature artichokes; 2 or 3 slices Italian salami or bologna, slivered and rinds removed; 6 to 8 fresh mushrooms, washed, drained, and slivered; 1 minced, canned pimiento; extra olives; anchovies; or whatever else you like.

Green Bean Salad (8 servings)

1 quart cooked shredded green beans (fresh or frozen)
2 green peppers, minced
1 cup diced celery
2 onions, peeled and minced
⅔ cup Traditional French Dressing (see recipe)
Salt and black pepper
Lettuce cups

Mix all ingredients lightly with two forks, adding more dressing if necessary. Chill well and serve in lettuce cups.

Variation: Chopped dill, parsley, chives, tarragon, basil, or any fresh herbs are a fine addition to this salad. If no fresh are handy, substitute a small amount of dried ones.

Green Bean and Mushroom Salad (8 servings)

Add ¼ pound of fresh mushrooms, washed, drained, and slivered, to the recipe above before refrigerating.

Russian Sauerkraut Salad (6 servings)

Jeannie and Paul Kolachov introduced me to this hearty, winter salad. It goes hand in glove with smoked meats and is equally at home with cold, sliced duck or goose.

1 pound fresh sauerkraut
Freshly-ground black pepper
1 medium onion, peeled and minced
4 tablespoons olive oil
Salt if needed

Cut sauerkraut into bits with scissors. Then mix all ingredients together and refrigerate an hour or so before serving.

Ante-Bellum Combination Salad (6 to 8 servings)

This used to be my favorite salad, although I find it a little sweet now. But don't cut down on the sugar—the results are not the same with less.

1 medium head firm cabbage
1 onion, peeled and grated
1 cup white or cider vinegar
1 tablespoon celery seed
1 green pepper, diced (optional)
1 cup sugar
1 tablespoon dry mustard
1 teaspoon salt or more
¼ teaspoon black pepper
Lettuce

Remove core and wilted leaves from cabbage. Shred cabbage as fine as possible. There should be 4 or 5 cups. Soak in ice water for 20 minutes to "crispen." Drain well, pat dry with a towel. Place in a bowl and mix with all other ingredients. Serve surrounded by lettuce leaves.

Cucumber-stuffed Tomatoes with Water-Cress Dressing (6 servings)

6 medium tomatoes, peeled
1 cup creamed cottage cheese
4 tablespoons minced celery
1 tablespoon chopped chives or green shallot tops
¼ cup mayonnaise or more
1 cucumber, peeled, shredded, and squeezed dry
1 small onion, peeled and grated
1 tablespoon minced parsley
Salt, pepper, Tabasco to taste
Few drops green coloring (optional)
Paprika for garnish

Cut tomatoes halfway through making an X. Open out gently; be careful not to break off sections. Mix other ingredients except garnish together, making a paste stiff enough to hold up, but not dry. Taste for seasoning, stuff into tomatoes, garnish with paprika; surround with lettuce or water cress. Serve with:

Water-Cress Dressing

½ cup minced water cress
½ cup chili sauce
½ cup Traditional French Dressing (see recipe)
Salt and black pepper

Combine all the ingredients and serve.

Poivrade Sauce (6 servings)

This recipe for cold artichokes, asparagus, broccoli, etc., is from Mrs. Hannah Glasse's almost priceless *The Art of Cookery Made Plain and Easy.* (A first edition, 1747, recently sold for $300 at a New York auction.) This, incidentally, was the only salad in her book. The dressing is sufficient for 6 cooked, chilled artichokes, 1½ pounds fresh asparagus or broccoli, or 2 (10-ounce) packages frozen, cooked, drained, and cooled.

4 anchovy fillets, mashed
4 tablespoons olive or salad oil
4 to 6 tablespoons wine, cider, or malt vinegar
4 shallots, shredded
2 teaspoons prepared mustard
2 tablespoons minced parsley
Salt and pepper
Dash Tabasco or pepper sauce

Mix all ingredients together, correct seasoning if necessary. This can be prepared ahead, put in a jar with a tight-fitting lid, and refrigerated until time to serve.

Zucchini à la Grecque (6 servings)

3 cups tender zucchini, sliced ¼ inch thick
2 sprigs tarragon, minced
2 sprigs parsley, minced
2 sprigs thyme, minced
½ teaspoon salt or more
⅛ teaspoon black pepper
Dash red pepper
1 bay leaf
1 tablespoon lemon or lime juice or more
¼ cup olive or salad oil
1 garlic clove, slivered
¼ teaspoon sugar
1 cup water or more

Put all ingredients in a saucepan. Cover, bring to a hard boil, turn heat low, and simmer 15 to 20 minutes. When zucchini is done, cool and refrigerate. A delicious salad or hors d'oeuvre.

Note: If fresh herbs are not available, substitute ½ teaspoon mixed dried herbs.

Plantation Potato Salad (6 servings)

6 small potatoes
Plantation Boiled Dressing
¼ cup chopped celery
¼ cup chopped parsley
Salt and pepper
1 small onion, peeled and minced
2 tablespoons chopped green pepper
1 tablespoon chopped pimiento (optional)
2 hard-cooked eggs, diced
Lettuce
Paprika for garnishing

Boil potatoes, cool, and peel; then slice thin. Make dressing and combine with other ingredients. Mix all together except garnish and lettuce. The salad should be moist but not runny. Serve in a pottery bowl, surround with lettuce leaves, and dust with paprika.

Plantation Boiled Dressing

2 eggs
1 rounded tablespoon flour
1 teaspoon salt
1 tablespoon sugar
¼ teaspoon dry mustard
¼ cup cider vinegar
1 tablespoon melted butter or olive oil
¼ cup water
3 tablespoons sweet or sour cream

Beat eggs well. Add dry ingredients and continue beating—an electric mixer helps. Pour in liquids except cream, slowly beating all the while. Cook in top of a double boiler until thick, stirring constantly, preferably with a wooden spoon. If mixture lumps, remove from heat and beat smooth again. Add cream; beat until fluffy. Use as soon as made or refrigerate in a covered jar. It will last several days.

Plantation Cabbage Salad (6 servings)

Mix 2 or 3 cups finely-shredded cabbage, soaked ½ hour in ice water, then drained, with the Plantation Boiled Dressing above. Chill before serving.

Swedish Herring Salad (6 to 8 servings)

This is an important item on any Swedish smörgåsbord table.

1 herring, canned in brine
1 cup Scandinavian Spiced Beets (see recipe)
1 cup cooked diced potatoes
2 or 3 tablespoons minced dill pickle
1 apple, pared and shredded
1 small onion, peeled and grated
Black pepper to taste
2 hard-cooked eggs, chopped
2 tablespoons minced parsley
Parsley for garnish

Drain herring and mince fine. Mix with other ingredients. Put in a small bowl and press down with back of a spoon to solidify. Refrigerate several hours. Loosen edges, turn out on a platter, and surround with a wreath of parsley.

MAIN-DISH SALADS

Perhaps the depression of 1930 contributed to the shift of salads from being a "mess of greens" to main-dish importance, salad ingredients being inexpensive as a rule. The calorie-conscious public probably completed its status.

Lady Morphy wrote these words of praise in her *Recipes of All Nations,* published in England just prior to World War II: "The Americans seem to be more creative in the invention of fancy mixed salads than in almost any other branch of the culinary art . . . They have a great variety of salad dressings . . . both unusual and attractive, and their poultry and shellfish salads are among the best in the world."

Whipped Salmon Mousse (8 Servings)

Here is another original from Marion Green's kitchen—the artist, her cook, David Minefield. This aspic makes a first-class hors d'oeuvre or canapé spread as well as a delicious salad.

1-pound can red Alaskan salmon
1 tablespoon gelatin
1 can (1¼ cups) consommé
1 teaspoon Worcestershire sauce
1 small onion, peeled and grated
1 cup mayonnaise
1 tablespoon tarragon vinegar or more
Juice of 1 lemon
Dash soy sauce
Dash Tabasco
Salt and black pepper to taste

Drain salmon well, remove skin and bones, and set aside. Soften gelatin in ¼ cup cold consommé; then place over hot water until gelatin melts. (*If you do not use consommé which jells when chilled, or if you substitute homemade stock, use an extra tablespoon of gelatin.*) And "bought" mayonnaise may require extra seasonings.

Beat all ingredients or whip in a blender until they are smooth and fluffy. Pour into a lightly-greased 1½-quart mold or in 8 individual molds. Or use jelly glasses or custard cups. Refrigerate until firm. Unmold, surround with lettuce leaves, water cress, or endive.

Garibaldi Supper Salad (1 serving)

This salad, originated by Louisville's Tosca Garibaldi, is often served at private clubs and restaurants throughout Kentucky. Try it for a cocktail-supper out on the terrace. Prepare individual portions in old-fashioned soup bowls or use foil pie pans.

¼ head iceberg lettuce
1 small head Bibb lettuce or few leaves Boston lettuce
1 hard-cooked egg, quartered
1 ripe tomato, peeled and quartered
½ cup diced baked chicken
¼ cup crumbled crisp bacon
2 tablespoons French dressing
2 tablespoons Roquefort or Danish Bleu Dressing (see recipe)

To make one serving, shred iceberg lettuce into soup bowl or pie pan. Place Bibb or Boston lettuce around the edge. Then alternate quarters of egg and tomato over the lettuce, making a circle. Pile chicken in the center. Top with bacon and dribble both dressings over all.

Chicken Salmagundi (8 servings)

This is my adaptation of a recipe in Mrs. Martha Bradley's *British Housewife,* (1755). It is a most distinctive chicken salad and one of the prettiest. Cook the chicken according to her directions given in Spiced Jellied Chicken Soup (see recipe).

5- to 6-pound chicken, cooked
½ lemon thinly-sliced, seeds removed
8 hard-cooked egg whites, riced (optional)
1-pound can small boiled onions (about)
1 cup Tarragon French Dressing (see recipe)
4 eggs, cooked 15 minutes
1 teaspoon Made Mustard *
1 tablespoon lemon juice
4 anchovy fillets or 1 teaspoon anchovy paste
1 tablespoon chopped parsley
John Evelyn's 1699 Dressing
Bibb lettuce or water cress
Extra anchovy fillets

Let chicken cool in strained broth. Remove skin. Cut breast in finger-length strips, ½ inch wide; wrap and set aside. Mince all remaining chicken, chop with lemon slices, or grind together using finest blade of meat grinder. I add the egg whites left from the dressing below, but the original did not.

Marinate onions overnight in Tarragon French Dressing. Drain and reserve dressing. Mash 4 egg yolks; blend, one ingredient at a time, mustard, lemon juice, anchovy fillets or paste, and parsley. Stuff into whites.

To assemble the salad: Put chopped chicken, mixed with John Evelyn's 1699 Dressing in a salad bowl; smooth with back of spoon. Surround with lettuce or water cress. Make spokes of a wheel alternating strips of chicken breast with extra anchovy fillets. Outline rim of bowl with onions. Place stuffed eggs in the center. Serve Tarragon French Dressing with the Salmagundi.

John Evelyn's 1699 Dressing

8 hard-cooked egg yolks
1 teaspoon salt
1 tablespoon sugar
1 tablespoon Made Mustard *
½ cup chicken fat or olive oil
¾ cup cider vinegar

Mash yolks to a paste with salt, sugar, and mustard. When smooth, add fat slowly, then the vinegar. Mix well.

Chicken Ring with Vegetable Salad (8 to 10 servings)

4- to 6-pound hen, boiled, or 3 or 4 cups cooked shredded chicken
1 cup finely-chopped celery
1 canned pimiento, chopped
1 green pepper, chopped
2¼ cups strained chicken broth
1 tablespoon gelatin
Juice of ½ lemon
Salt and pepper to taste
Tabasco

To the shredded chicken, add celery, pimiento, green pepper, and 1 cup broth. Soften gelatin in ¼ cup cold broth and dissolve in 1 cup boiling broth; add in lemon juice. Stir until thoroughly smooth, strain if any lumps. Combine with chicken mixture and taste for seasoning. Pour into a lightly-greased ring mold. Refrigerate until firm—preferably overnight. At serving time, unmold on a round platter. Surround with lettuce or water cress and fill center with:

Vegetable Salad

2 ripe tomatoes, peeled and cut in eighths
1 cucumber, peeled and diced
4 small spring onions, minced
6 radishes, sliced thin
1 green pepper, minced
½ cup finely-minced celery
½ cup cooked green beans
½ cup cooked green peas
½ cup cooked sliced carrots
1 cup Garlic Dressing (see recipe)

Marinate vegetables in the highly-seasoned dressing at least an hour before serving. Drain and put in center of Chicken Ring. Use traditional French Dressing or a herbed dressing for the marinade if you wish. Serve with the marinade or:

Seneca Dressing

2 cups tart mayonnaise, made with lime instead of lemon juice
½ cup chili sauce
2 tablespoons chopped chives
2 tablespoons chopped water cress
2 tablespoons caviar (domestic)
2 hard-cooked eggs, riced
Salt and pepper
Tabasco

Mix all the ingredients together; pour into a serving bowl.

Note: Cook chicken according to directions in Spiced Jellied Chicken Soup or use an extra tablespoon gelatin in preparing chicken ring.

Deviled Cheese Aspic (8 to 10 servings)

This delightful and very rich salad used to be served when I was a child. It can be made a day ahead; in fact it's better if this is done. Turn the aspic out on a large round silver or china platter covered with water cress or shredded iceberg lettuce. Surround with slivers of avocado and grapefruit sections. Fill the center with seedless grapes or green winter grapes, peeled and seeded. Or use any fruit in season, peaches and plums, for instance, or melon balls, or pears. It is an impressive dessert salad too. Here's Mina Cole's recipe.

3 tablespoons mayonnaise
1 tablespoon Worcestershire sauce
1 tablespoon walnut sauce or catsup
1 tablespoon tomato catsup
5 (3-ounce) packages cream cheese
1 tablespoon gelatin
3 tablespoons cold water
2 cups heavy cream, whipped
¼ cup diced green pepper
12 salted almonds
2 dozen green olives, seeded and chopped
3 tablespoons minced celery
Traditional French Dressing (see recipe)

Gradually combine mayonnaise, Worcestershire, walnut and tomato catsup with softened cream cheese. Mash with a fork or blend with an electric mixer. Mix gelatin in a cup with cold water and cook over hot water until gelatin melts. Then add to cheese mixture. Fold in whipped cream and all other ingredients, correcting seasoning if necessary. Pour into a lightly-greased ring mold and refrigerate until firm, preferably overnight. Serve the Traditional French Dressing sans garlic or onion.

FRUIT COMBINATIONS

Serve any tart dressing in the Salad Make-Up (but omit garlic or onion) with the fruit salads given below.

Alternate sections of orange, grapefruit, tangerine, and avocado, and top with slivered, fresh, hothouse mushrooms. This is especially good with Whipped Cream and Horse-Radish Mayonnaise.

A combination of fresh sliced strawberries and fresh pineapple chunks makes a wonderful dessert salad when served with French dressing, sweetened with 2 tablespoons melted tart jelly for every cup of dressing.

Make a midsummer combination of peaches, plums, pears, nectarines, and apricots. Place in a circle over shredded lettuce and pile pomegranate seeds in the center.

SALAD MAKE-UP

Garlic Oil

Use this California "find" sparingly—it's potent! Put 12 cloves garlic, peeled and split, in a pint jar with 2 cups pure olive oil or 1½ cups salad oil and ½ cup olive oil. Cover. Leave for 10 days then strain oil into another jar and cover. (Garlic spoils if left too long.) Use in any dressing or sauce that calls for oil and garlic.

Salad-Dressing Mix (Basic recipe)

Here is a revolutionary salad mix, enough for 6 cups of dressing. It has been a boon to me and I hope it will be for you.

2 tablespoons salt
2 tablespoons dry mustard
1 tablespoon garlic powder
1 tablespoon onion powder
1 teaspoon black pepper
½ teaspoon red pepper
1 teaspoon paprika
1 teaspoon red chili powder

Sift all ingredients into a bowl and stir well. Use a mortar and pestle if you have one. Store in a jar with a tight lid.

Traditional French Dressing (6 servings)

1 tablespoon Salad-Dressing Mix
⅓ cup cider or wine vinegar
⅔ cup olive or salad oil
1 teaspoon sugar or ¼ grain saccharine (optional)

Put dry ingredients on top of vinegar and oil. Whip well or use electric mixer. Or put liquid ingredients in a bottle, add the dry, and shake well. (If you want a sweet dressing, mix sugar or saccharine with vinegar before making dressing.)

Garlic Dressing (6 servings)

Use 2 tablespoons Garlic Oil when measuring oil for Traditional French Dressing. Or add 1 or 2 split cloves of garlic to dressing in jar. If you prefer a slightly sweet dressing, rub a split clove of garlic over a lump of sugar. When essence is absorbed, drop sugar lump into dressing jar and shake to dissolve.

Tarragon French Dressing (6 servings)

Add 2 or more teaspoons chopped fresh tarragon to Traditional French Dressing, or ½ teaspoon dried. Make other herbed dressings using dill, thyme, etc., in same amount. Or use Herb Vinegars (see recipes).

Henry Bane Dressing (8 to 10 servings)

Add ⅓ cup Henry Bane Sauce (see recipe) to Traditional French Dressing and shake well.

India Relish and Hard-cooked Egg Dressing (8 to 10 servings)

Combine ⅓ cup India relish, 1 riced hard-cooked egg, 2 tablespoons minced, green pepper, 2 tablespoons minced, canned pimiento, 2 tablespoons minced chives or shallots, 2 tablespoons minced parsley with Traditional French Dressing. Delicious on sections of iceberg lettuce.

Hawaiian Pineapple-and-Ginger Dressing (8 servings)

Add 1 cup of crushed pineapple with juice and 2 tablespoons preserved or candied ginger, minced, to Traditional French Dressing.

Roquefort or Danish Bleu Dressing (6 to 8 servings)

Mash ¼ pound Roquefort or Danish Bleu cheese to a paste with a little Traditional French Dressing, then beat in remaining dressing.

Vermouth Dressing (8 servings)

Add ⅓ cup dry vermouth to Traditional French Dressing and omit sugar or saccharine as wine is a little sweet.

Vinaigrette Sauce (4 to 6 servings)

Arrange serving portions of drained, cooked vegetables on a salad dish, surround with lettuce or water cress and top with a generous amount of sauce. This amount of sauce is enough for 2 (10-ounce) packages frozen asparagus, broccoli, etc.

1 hard-cooked egg, riced
1 tablespoon minced parsley
1 tablespoon chopped dill pickle
1 teaspoon salt or more
¼ teaspoon paprika
¼ teaspoon black pepper
1 tablespoon minced pimiento
1 teaspoon chopped chives or green onion tops
1 tablespoon tarragon wine vinegar
½ cup Traditional French Dressing
1 tablespoon minced green pepper

Mix ingredients. Serve cold or heat in top of a double boiler over low heat, stirring occasionally. Do not boil. Serve over vegetables.

Mayonnaise (8 servings)

1 whole egg
1 egg yolk
1½ teaspoons Salad-Dressing Mix
1½ cups salad or olive oil
1 tablespoon lime or lemon juice
1 teaspoon strong wine vinegar

I use an electric mixer to make this mayonnaise. Put eggs in a small bowl and whip well with the dressing mix. Then slowly pour on the oil, only a thin stream at first, then gradually more until the mayonnaise thickens considerably. Add a little lime or lemon juice and more oil, *never stop whipping,* then some vinegar, and more oil and so on until ingredients are combined. This makes 1½ cups of stiff and very delicious mayonnaise.

To prevent curdling: Have all ingredients at room temperature before making mayonnaise. If it does curdle, take another egg and gradually add the curdled mixture to the egg, a little at a time. It will come out smooth.

Garlic Mayonnaise (8 servings)

Substitute 2 tablespoons Garlic Oil (see recipe above) for some of the oil used in making Mayonnaise, or crush a small clove into the finished mayonnaise and whip well. The flavor improves with standing.

Caper Mayonnaise (6 servings)

To every cup Garlic Mayonnaise, add 1 or 2 tablespoons of capers.

Green Mayonnaise (6 servings)

To every cup Mayonnaise add 1 tablespoon each: minced chives or green shallot tops, parsley, a teaspoon of fresh, minced tarragon, thyme, dill, or any herb desired. Use ¼ teaspoon dried herbs when fresh are not handy.

Whipped Cream and Horse-Radish Mayonnaise (6 to 8 servings)

To make this delicious combination, mix ½ cup mayonnaise with ½ cup whipped sweet or sour cream, and add 2 tablespoons prepared horse-radish or more to taste.

Sauce Remoulade (6 servings)

2 hard-cooked egg yolks
2 or 3 anchovy fillets
1 cup Garlic Mayonnaise
1 teaspoon curry powder or more
1 teaspoon minced chives
½ teaspoon French mustard
2 teaspoons finely-minced shallots
2 teaspoons finely-minced capers
1 teaspoon grated onion, juice and pulp
2 teaspoons minced parsley

Mash egg yolks well with anchovies. Add mayonnaise slowly to make a smooth paste. Add all other ingredients. Beat well or whip in a blender. Store in a jar with a tight-fitting lid. Refrigerate until ready to serve.

Green Goddess Dressing (About 1 pint)

This is Genevieve Callahan's version of the most famous and popular salad served at the Palace Hotel in San Francisco. It was first concocted when George Arliss was appearing in the play, *The Green Goddess.*

1 clove garlic, grated
3 tablespoons finely-chopped anchovies or anchovy paste
3 tablespoons finely-chopped chives or green onions
1 tablespoon lemon juice
3 tablespoons tarragon wine vinegar
½ cup heavy cream (preferably soured)
1 cup mayonnaise
⅓ cup finely-chopped parsley
Salt and coarse black pepper

Combine ingredients in order given. Chill, then pour liberally over coarsely-torn mixed greens—romaine, chicory, and escarole, or head lettuce and leaf lettuce. Toss until well coated, adding more salt and pepper as needed. Serve in individual plates or bowls to accompany the main course.

17 CORNUCOPIA OF FRUIT

Fruit makes a beautiful table decoration for a cocktail-supper—and it can also be your dessert. Arrange the colorful pieces, chosen for variety of forms, in a cornucopia, an epergne or bowl, or on a tray; pile them high in the center, and let them spill over the sides onto the tablecloth. In winter, you might use oranges, tangerines, winter apples, and pears, accented with bunches of grapes and raisins and a scattering of nuts in the shell. In summer, the choice is unlimited: peaches, still with a faint bloom; red and purple plums; golden nectarines, slightly-rouged; cherries, black and red; a pineapple with stylish topknot; jade-green seedless grapes, and strawberries with their little skull caps intact.

For what many of us consider the perfect dessert, serve with your cornucopia of fruit a tray of assorted cheeses and crackers—water biscuits, split, buttered, and toasted, or cross crackers.

FRESH FRUIT DESSERTS

Midsummer Fruit Mélange

Combine peeled, sliced peaches; nectarines; greengage, red, and blue plums; blueberries; raspberries or any other berry in season; pears, cored and peeled; seedless grapes or any other fresh fruits with Sugar Sirup (see recipe below). An orange cordial, Cointreau or Triple Sec or curaçao, is a delightful addition—3 to 4 tablespoons to a quart of fruit.

Tropical Fruit Cup

When exotic fruits are on the market, no cocktail-supper dessert is more pleasing than this combination: mangoes and papayas, peeled and sliced; pineapple, cut in chunks; blueberries; and red cherries, pitted. Add Sugar Sirup to taste and the juice of half a lime; it brings out the flavors. A few tablespoons of light rum, kirsch, Southern Comfort, or an apricot liqueur are recommended.

Winter Compote

Pared, cored, sliced apples, grapefruit, orange, and tangerine sections, peeled and all membrane removed, and a sliced banana if you like, with a garnish of pomegranate seeds makes a classic winter dessert. Add Sugar Sirup to taste and blend with a liqueur.

Sugar Sirup

Boil 1 cup sugar with 1 cup water until slightly thickened, 4 or 5 minutes. Cool, pour into a jar with a tight lid. This keeps indefinitely when refrigerated. For variety, cook ½ lemon, juice and rind, with the sugar and water, and let the rind cool in the sirup. Strain before storing.

To use: 1 cup should be sufficient for 1 quart of prepared cut fruit. (This will serve 8 generously.) The amount of sirup will depend on your taste and sweetness of fruit.

Melon Shells

A slice of melon makes a fine ending to a summer meal. Scooped-out watermelons or cantaloupe halves are pretty containers for a mixture of fruit, especially Midsummer Fruit Mélange or Tropical Fruit Cup, or melon balls.

Minted Melon Balls

Melon balls, soaked in a little lime juice and Sugar Sirup for half an hour or so, then piled into glasses and sprinkled lightly with chopped mint, make a fine summer dessert.

Melon Ka-Bobs

Alternate cubes of watermelon, cantaloupe, honeydew, and Persian melon on wooden skewers and serve for outdoor cocktail-suppers. Do not put the melon cubes on until just ready to serve.

Tipsy Melon

To infuse liquor without cutting the melon (a solid melon like watermelon), I've found a large, 50 cc., medical syringe with a long needle very useful. Insert the needle at 3- or 4-inch intervals, as far as it will go, and squirt out small amounts of liquor until all has been used. Or, if the melon is hollow like a honeydew, you can cut off the top, empty the juices and scrape out the seeds. Then stand the melon on the uncut end in a bowl which will keep it upright; you might have to pack papers around it. Fill melon with liquor and secure the lid with picks.

Watermelon with White Wine

Infuse about 2 cups of white wine (or champagne!) in an average-sized watermelon, using the syringe method given above. Refrigerate overnight or at least 12 hours. Cut in sections to serve.

Honeydew with Cointreau

Prepare as directed for hollow melons. Use 2 or 3 ounces Cointreau or Grand Marnier, secure top with picks, and refrigerate 12 hours or overnight. To serve, pour liqueur into a pitcher, and pass with the melon cut into sections.

Cantaloupe with Anis or Port

The Spaniards are very fond of using anis liqueur with melons, or port is good, too. Follow the recipe for Honeydew with Cointreau substituting anis or port.

Note: Sherry is a delicious addition to a melon. Try it in a Persian melon. Light rum, kirsch, or any brandy can be used effectively, and all the preparation is done ahead.

Pineapple Shells with Fruit

Cut a pineapple in half, lengthwise, scoop out the pineapple leaving a half-inch-thick shell. Fill with one of the fruit compotes above, with or without liquor. Top, as the Hawaiians do, with a scoop of fruit sherbert or water ice.

Snow Grapes (8 servings)

Mary Snow Abbott gave this delightful recipe. It is economical, too, when seedless green grapes are in season. Allow 1½ to 1¾ pounds grapes (weighed before removing stems). Wash and drain, then separate grapes from stems. Mix with 2 cups sour cream and sweeten to taste with ¾ to 1 cup brown sugar. Chill thoroughly. Serve in a large bowl or in individual dishes.

Another method of preparing this dessert, suited especially to a fall evening, is to mix the sour cream and grapes, chill; then just before serving, sprinkle about an inch of brown sugar over the bowl or dishes, place under the grill until sugar melts and bubbles. Watch that it does not burn. This forms a pretty glaze over the cold grapes.

Fruit Fools (6 servings)

The British love this dessert. It is good and so simple to prepare. Mix equal parts of well-chilled Red Raspberry Purée or other fruit purée or fresh fruit, and cold boiled custard or whipped cream. Pile into sherbet glasses and refrigerate until serving time.

Red Raspberry Purée

Prepare

2 cups of berries, add about ½ cup sugar, a teaspoon of lemon juice for tartness if you wish, and put through a food mill or blender. To remove seeds, force through a strainer. Makes 1 cup. A pretty topping for puddings and frozen desserts.

Note: Prepare sliced strawberries, peeled, sliced peaches or apricots the same way.

COOKED FRUIT DESSERTS

Gala Baked Apple (6 servings)

Baked winter apples make fine cocktail-supper desserts. Prepare 6 apples, core them, and pare if you wish. Fill with a mixture of sugar and cinnamon, or nuts and raisins, or tart jelly or mincemeat, and place in a shallow baking dish with 2 cups Sugar Sirup (recipe on page 204) poured over them. Bake 45 minutes to an hour in a 350° F. oven, or until tender and transparent. Turn once if unpared. Baste often if pared. Serve plain, with boiled custard, vanilla pudding, or whipped cream.

Baked-Apple Meringues (6 servings)

Use 6 apples, baked without skins, stuffed or not as you wish, and cooled. Place each on a thin round of sponge or poundcake the same width as the apple. Make a heavy meringue: beat 4 egg whites with a few grains of salt until stiff—an electric mixer helps, then slowly add 1 cup sugar, 1 teaspoon vanilla, and 1 teaspoon mild vinegar. Pile this thickly over the apples insulating them well. Put in a hot oven, 450° F., for 6 to 8 minutes or until meringue turns a faint caramel color. Let apples stand at room temperature until ready to serve.

Spiced Fruit in Wine (6 servings)

This can be cooked either on top of the stove or baked in the oven; either is successful. For a winter version: Use 2 pears, peeled, cored, and cut in half; 2 pared, cored apples, cut in half or quartered; 1 cup seedless green grapes. For summer: Use 3 peeled, halved peaches or pears; 1 cup sweet red cherries, pitted; 3 red or blue plums; 3 apricots, peeled and seeds removed. Or use any selection of fruit you prefer.

Wine Sauce:

1 cup Sugar Sirup (see recipe)
1 cup red wine
6 whole cloves
6 allspice berries
1 large stick cinnamon
¼ lemon, cut in thin rings, seeds removed
½ teaspoon whole coriander seeds (optional)
Few grains salt

Mix the Sugar Sirup with red wine thoroughly. Add other ingredients, pour over prepared fruit. For top of the stove, bring sirup to a boil, reduce heat, and simmer 10 to 20 minutes, or bake in a casserole 20 to 30 minutes in a 350° F. oven. Time varies according to ripeness of the fruit. When fruit is tender, serve warm, or cool and refrigerate. It keeps well under refrigeration.

Hot Fruit Compote (8 servings)

This is another good-tasting winter dessert and a nice one to prepare in your chafing dish. Fix a quart of drained fruit ahead of time. Use a combination of canned or frozen fruits mixed with fresh grapefruit or orange sections (all membrane removed). Put in a serving bowl and add liqueur to taste—2 to 4 tablespoons. At dessert time, heat the juices in the chafing dish. (There should be 1½ to 2 cups; if not, make up the difference with orange or grapefruit juice.) Add ¼ cup currant jelly, or peach or apricot preserves, or marmalade. When the juice boils and jelly or preserves melt, pour over the fruit. Serve at once, plain, with whipped cream, or boiled custard.

1830 Orange Compote (6 servings)

I found this recipe in a cookbook published in 1830; it is the most outstanding orange sauce I ever tasted. Serve it on custard or any plain cake or pudding, or spoon generously over Rice Imperial (see recipe).

3 large oranges
½ cup water
½ cup sugar
¼ cup apricot or peach preserves or marmalade
2 tablespoons curaçao
2 tablespoons Grand Marnier or Cointreau
Few grains salt

Peel oranges down to the pulp and put peeling in a saucepan with water and sugar. Remove orange pulp from membrane saving all juices. When sugar sirup boils hard, let boil 2 minutes longer. Strain over pulp and juice. Return to heat and boil 2 minutes longer. Add preserves or marmalade and cool. Add liqueurs and salt. This can be made several days ahead and refrigerated until serving time. Keep covered.

Stewed Damson Plums (8 servings)

Buy 1 quart damson plums (measured before stoning). Cut in half, remove stone, put in a saucepan with 1 cup sugar, ½ cup water, and 1 stick cinnamon. Cook until plums are tender, from 10 to 20 minutes. Chill and serve; use as a colorful topping for English Cold Shape or Rice Imperial (see recipes).

Cardinal Peaches (8 servings)

Simmer 4 large peeled, fresh ripe peaches or pears, pitted or cored and cut in half, in 1 cup Sugar Sirup (see recipe). You can use 1 inch of vanilla bean or 1 teaspoon of extract instead of the lemon flavoring if you wish. When tender, remove from heat and cool in the sirup. Just before serving, drain, and place around a mold of Rice Imperial or a Cold Shape (see recipes) on a serving platter. Coat each piece of fruit with strawberry or Red Raspberry Purée (see recipe). Or put a scoop of vanilla or bisque ice cream on the fruit and pour a purée over. To garnish the way the French originators do, sprinkle with blanched, slivered, toasted almonds.

FRUIT IN GOOD SPIRITS

Party Fruit

Canned or frozen fruits can be transformed from an everyday to a party dessert by marinating them in spirits or cordials a few hours. Here are several suggestions: pineapple in crème de menthe or kirsch; peaches in Southern Comfort, Apri, or Grand Marnier; pears in port or red wine; cherries in kirsch or Cherry Heering. Serve well chilled. Spoon over pieces of angel cake, torn with two forks, or sautéed poundcake. It's a Louisville specialty to serve pineapple in crème de menthe over vanilla ice cream and angel cake—or over lemon sherbet.

Fruit Flambé (8 servings)

At the cocktail-buffet it is fun to flame fruit toppings for ice-cream desserts right at the table. Here is the basic recipe.

1/4 cup butter
1/4 cup sugar or 1/4 cup sugar and 1/4 cup fruit preserves, jam, or jelly
2 ounces light rum, kirsch, brandy, applejack, or whisky
2 ounces liqueur
Fresh fruit for 8

In the chafing dish, melt butter and add sugar and preserves if using them. Cook until well blended and thick, then add 1 ounce of the stronger spirits and 1 ounce liqueur. Mix in the fruit, cook until tender, allowing at least 1½ to 2 minutes on each side. Turn fruit once, or stir cut-up fruits or berries. Add rest of spirits and liqueur, remove from heat, stir a few seconds to warm, then ignite. Tilt the pan back and forth until the flame dies—more effective in subdued light. Then spoon over ice cream and serve.

Combinations of Fruit to Flame

Allow a half a peach or a whole one to each guest. Cook as directed, using French brandy or Southern Comfort and curaçao or Cointreau. Good on vanilla ice cream.

Flame apricots, allowing 2 to each serving, peeled or not as you wish. Cook as above, using French brandy and Apri or any apricot liqueur. Serve over coconut ice cream.

Pineapple, fresh or canned, and fresh strawberries make a heavenly combination to flame with brandy or kirsch and Grand Marnier or Cointreau.

For bananas, use rum and curaçao or Triple Sec or just plain bourbon whisky. I usually add a dash of cinnamon and a grating of nutmeg. Allow one to a person, cut in quarters if large. Serve over vanilla or coffee ice cream.

FRUIT SOUPS

In Scandinavian countries, fruit soups are a popular first course. In this country, we usually serve them at the end of the meal. As the old gamblers used to say, "You pays your money and you takes your choice."

Red Raspberry Soup (8 to 10 servings)

I had this at a small Danish Restaurant, served *after* the smörgåsbord, probably to please the Americans. It was brought to the table in small glass punch cups with a pitcher of thick cream. I'm sure the pale ruby color had been reinforced with a few drops of coloring. Do likewise if your raspberries begin to fade.

1 cup water
1 cup sugar
1 quart red raspberries
1 tablespoon cornstarch
Few drops red coloring (optional)

Boil water and sugar in a large skillet or Dutch oven. When thickened, after about 4 minutes, add washed, drained berries. Simmer 2 or 3 minutes or until thoroughly heated and permeated with the sirup. Add cornstarch, mixed with a little cold water, and cook 1 minute. Remove from heat, add coloring if desired, cool, and serve as above.

Swedish Spiced Dried Fruit Soup (8 servings)

This is one of the most valuable winter desserts I have in my recipe files.

1 pound mixed dried fruit: prunes, apricots, peaches, pears, etc.
2 cups red wine
6 cups water
1 lemon, sliced thin
1 cup sugar
Few grains salt
1 blade mace or 1/8 teaspoon ground
2 sticks cinnamon or 1/2 teaspoon ground
2 whole cloves or 1/8 teaspoon ground
2 allspice berries or 1/8 teaspoon ground
1/4 teaspoon grated nutmeg
1 whole cardamom seed (optional)
1/4 teaspoon ground coriander seeds (optional)

Put all ingredients in a soup kettle, cover tightly, and let simmer until fruit is done. If fruits are soaked overnight or a few hours, they will cook in 1/2 hour; otherwise it will take an hour. Taste for seasonings, adding more sugar or spices if necessary.

Variations: I like to add a pint of sour red cherries to this soup; use sweetened canned or frozen ones. Also I add in any opened jars of jellies or preserves when the soup is hot, stirring until dissolved. Peach preserves, pear, strawberry, or apricot, all seem to blend. To stretch the soup, remember you can serve two more with every extra cup of ingredients you add.

Note: I do not thicken this soup but the Swedes do. If you want, add 2 tablespoons pink sago or quick-cooking tapioca to the cooked soup and continue cooking until the thickening agent is done. Or 1 1/2 tablespoons of cornstarch mixed with 3 tablespoons of cold water will also thicken the soup in about 2 minutes.

18 SUGAR TALK

This chapter is particularly for those who still believe that the crowning glory of a supper party is a really good homemade dessert. If your cocktail-supper has been quite filling, you may want to serve Jellied Zabaglione or French Strawberry Pudding. If lighter fare has preceded the dessert, bring the meal to an elegant conclusion with the Bond Family Dessert Eggnog. For holidays, there are old favorites such as Sherried Charlotte Russe and Mother's Nesselrode Pudding. And there are a few new desserts to choose from which I hope will strike you as a happy ending to a pleasant meal.

FREEZE AND SERVE

I think a mousse is the most professional and successful form of frozen refrigerator dessert. It used to be necessary to pack it in a covered mold in salt and ice for hours. This method still works, but with a modern freezer the process is much simpler. Just pour the mousse into individual paper muffin cups, place them in the freezer, and they are firm in about an hour. If you have enough space, you can freeze a large mold also. This takes longer to harden. Cover the tops of the paper cups or mold securely with foil or freezer paper after the mousse hardens and keep until ready to serve, or store in freezer cartons.

Vanilla Mousse (8 servings)

The number of servings depends on the size of the paper cups. Whip a cup of heavy cream until stiff but not buttery; it is better to have it a little runny rather than too stiff. Add powdered sugar to taste, about 2 tablespoons, and ½ teaspoon vanilla extract or a few gratings from a vanilla bean. Pour into cups or a pint mold and freeze until firm. If not served the same day it is made, wrap in foil, or put in freezer cartons.

Burnt Almond Mousse (8 servings)

This old favorite dates back to the Gay Nineties. Add ½ cup ground burnt-almond candy to the Vanilla Mousse before freezing.

Foolproof Biscuit Tortoni (8 servings)

To the Vanilla Mousse, add ½ cup ground, blanched, toasted almonds or almond macaroon crumbs. Add 2 to 2½ tablespoons of sherry. Too much tends to make the cream separate when it freezes. Use a tablespoon or two more sugar if wine is dry. Pour mousse into individual paper cups. Sprinkle extra ground almonds or macaroon crumbs over the tops and garnish with half a crystallized cherry when mousse is firm enough.

French Chocolate Mousse (8 servings)

To the Vanilla Mousse, add 1 cup grated sweet or semisweet chocolate. Pour into individual containers or a pint mold. Sprinkle chocolate shavings over when firm enough. Put half a crystallized cherry or pineapple or a marron (preserved chestnut) in the center of each.

Chocolate Cases (10 to 12 cases)

For each case, use two fluted paper cups (the same size you need for mousse), one inside the other for extra stiffness. If the paper cups fit exactly into your muffin-pan cups, put them in after pouring the chocolate. Set in the freezer until chocolate is firm.

Melt 12 ounces semisweet chocolate in top of a double boiler with 1/4 cup butter or margarine. Stir well. Remove from heat, add 1/2 teaspoon vanilla, and let stand a moment to thicken. Make one case at a time. Coat the inside of each cup with chocolate. Make sides smooth using your fingers (as I do) or the back of a spoon. There must be no holes or breaks in the chocolate. Do not make walls too thin. As soon as cup is well coated, place in muffin pan if using, and set in the freezer on a flat surface. If chocolate gets too firm to handle, reheat it. Let cups remain in freezer until hard.

To remove paper, separate bottom of paper cup from the chocolate with the tip of a sharp knife. Be careful not to crack the case. Slit paper cup up one side and pull it away from the chocolate. Fill the chocolate cases with one of the mousses, freeze, and serve. This makes a *very* professional looking dessert.

Mother's Nesselrode Pudding (8 servings)

I can't find out whether Count Nesselrode, one of the dashing young officers with Alexander I of Russia, originated this dessert, or whether it was named for him by some tactful Parisian chef to gain favor with a conquering hero. But it did originate in Paris when the allied armies marched into that city after Napoleon's defeat in 1814. Here is my mother's version of this regal dessert.

Cook 25 to 30 large Italian chestnuts for 1 hour. Remove inner and outer skin; put through a food mill or ricer while still hot. This should make 1 cup of chestnut purée. Set aside.

2 egg yolks
3 tablespoons pineapple juice
½ teaspoon vanilla
½ cup sugar or more to taste
1 tablespoon rum or French brandy
1 cup chestnut purée
1 pint heavy cream
¼ cup chopped blanched almonds
¼ cup diced crystallized cherries
¼ cup diced crystallized pineapple

Beat egg yolks well. Add pineapple juice, vanilla, and sugar. Beat until thick and lemon-colored. Pour into double boiler and cook, stirring constantly, until sugar has dissolved and mixture is smooth. It should just coat the spoon; do not cook too long or it will curdle. Let cool, add rum or brandy (not too much or mixture will not freeze); fold in chestnut purée and whipped cream. Mix the chopped almonds and fruits and press them into the bottom and sides of a lightly-buttered mold. Mother used a 2-quart melon mold, but any shape will do that has a tight-fitting lid. Use a small loaf pan and make a top of heavy foil if you like. Pour pudding mixture into the prepared mold, cover, and place on a flat surface in the freezer. Leave until ready to serve. It should freeze in 3 or 4 hours, but it is safer to make and freeze the day before using.

Frozen Cottage Cheese Mousse (12 servings)

Mary Mack made this dessert on her Gateway television program. It is simply delicious and can be frozen in two refrigerator ice trays or in individual cups or tiny foil pans. I've made a few changes in her recipe but no basic ones. This is, incidentally, one of the least expensive mousses to make.

Crumb Mixture

2 cups zweibach crumbs
¼ cup sugar
¼ cup softened butter
½ teaspoon cinnamon

Mix all the ingredients. Save out ½ cup and divide the rest between 2 lightly-buttered ice trays, or put enough to cover the bottom and sides of buttered paper muffin cups or foil pans.

Cheese Mixture

1 pound homogenized cottage cheese
2 (3-ounce) packages cream cheese
1 cup sugar
Few grains salt
1 teaspoon vanilla
4 eggs, separated
1 cup heavy sweet or sour cream
Crystallized cherries for garnishing

If you have an electric mixer use it for this. Place everything except the egg whites and cream in a bowl and mix well. Then fold in well-beaten egg whites and whipped cream. Or mix the cream cheese with a little of the egg yolks to make a smooth paste free from lumps, combine with other ingredients, beaten egg whites and whipped cream last of all. Pour mixture into the trays or cups. Sprinkle with reserved crumbs—make an outline of the portions if you wish. When firm enough, press half a cherry in the center of each slice. Return to freezer until ready to serve.

Bond Family Dessert Eggnog (25 servings)

This recipe is an unusual holiday combination of rich eggnog with vanilla ice cream chopped into it, making a frappé consistency. Serve it in a punch bowl and ladle into little punch cups, ice cream bowls, or sherbet glasses. Grate nutmeg over each portion. Like many of my best recipes, this is from the Bond family's files.

1 dozen eggs
11 ounces French brandy (1¼ cups)
11 ounces bourbon whisky (1¼ cups)
1⅓ ounces rum (3 tablespoons)
1 gallon vanilla ice cream
Nutmeg

Beat eggs well using an electric mixer if possible. Slowly add liquor, almost drop by drop, as mixture is being beaten. Get another pair of hands to help you beat or pour if you don't have an electric mixer. This part can be done before the party as it does not hurt it to stand. Keep refrigerated until ready to use. Just at serving time stir mixture well and, using a sharp knife, cut the ice cream into the eggnog —it must be firm but not too hard to cut into small chunks. Let it blend in.

Ladle eggnog back and forth until sweet enough; it gets its sugar from the ice cream. Serve as directed above.

CHILL AND SERVE

Chocolate-Pecan Refrigerator Pudding (10 to 12 servings)

Geraldine Pope brought Louisville this recipe from Tenneille, Georgia. It can be made several days ahead. Top each serving with a spoonful of whipped cream as Geraldine does if you wish; I think it is rich enough as it is.

2 ounces (2 squares) bitter chocolate
½ cup granulated sugar
¼ cup water
4 eggs, separated
½ cup butter, softened
1 cup powdered sugar
1 tablespoon vanilla
Few grains salt
1 cup pecan halves
1½ dozen ladyfingers

Cook chocolate, granulated sugar, and water in top of a double boiler until chocolate melts. Stir smooth. Remove from heat; add in beaten egg yolks. Then cook until mixture coats the spoon, but not too thick—like a boiled custard. Set aside to cool. Cream butter with powdered sugar, using an electric mixer if handy. Add vanilla. Fold by hand into cooled chocolate mixture. Beat egg whites with salt until stiff and fold in. Then combine nuts. Have ready a pan, lined with waxed paper (see note) with split ladyfingers placed side by side across the *bottom* of the pan. (Do not put them on the sides.) Cover with a layer of chocolate. Make 3 layers of each with chocolate on top layer. Chill in the refrigerator. To serve, lift onto a platter, slice, and transfer to dessert plates.

Note: To line the pan, Geraldine uses a double fold of waxed paper across the bottom of a long tin loaf pan, and lets it extend a few inches beyond each end. This makes it easy to lift out chilled pudding top side up. The folded paper is covered with another sheet, fitted into the bottom and sides as snugly as possible.

Sherried Charlotte Russe (8 servings)

According to my husband, my mother-in-law served this dessert on very special occasions—a good cue to follow.

1 tablespoon gelatin
2 tablespoons cold water
3 eggs, separated
⅓ cup sugar or more to taste
Few grains salt
2 cups heavy cream
1 teaspoon vanilla
3 tablespoons sherry, rum, or bourbon whisky
1 dozen almond-paste macaroons

Soften gelatin in the cold water. Place container over hot water and cook until gelatin dissolves. Eggs should be separated when cold and allowed to reach room temperature, before beating. Beat yolks with sugar. Fold in whites, beaten stiff with salt. Add melted gelatin and work *quickly* to avoid lumps. Fold in whipped cream, vanilla, and sherry or liquor. Taste, adding more sugar or liquor if needed. Pour into serving bowl lined with macaroons and refrigerate. My mother-in-law always crumbled a few macaroons to sprinkle over the top after the dessert was firm enough. Any leftover macaroons can be pressed around the edges when mixture is almost set. Refrigerate until ready to serve.

English Cold Shape (6 servings)

This is the familiar blanc mange with an eighteenth-century touch. It is a very pretty dessert, which, when flavored with orange flower water and rose water, and topped with a fruit sauce, tastes so unusual, you'll find it an ideal way to end a modern cocktail-supper. You can purchase those flavorings at drugstores. If you can't find them I've suggested substitutions.

1 pint cream
5 tablespoons sugar
2 tablespoons cold water
1 tablespoon gelatin
Few grains salt
½ teaspoon orange flower water or use almond extract
½ teaspoon rose water or use vanilla extract

Put cream in a double boiler. Heat to boiling but do not allow to boil. Add sugar and remove from stove. Mix water with gelatin and add to hot cream. Stir until dissolved; strain if necessary. Add salt and flavorings. Pour into melon mold or 6 individual molds very lightly brushed with olive oil. Cool and refrigerate until firm—overnight is best. Turn out on a platter with sides or use a shallow bowl. Pour sweetened strawberries or raspberries, a fruit purée, Cardinal Peaches or Pears, Stewed Damson Plums, or Spiced Fruit in Wine Sauce around the dessert. All fruit-sauce recipes will be found in the Cornucopia of Fruit chapter.

Sherry-and-Brandy Jelly (10 to 12 servings)

Jane McFerran is to be thanked for this wonderful dessert. Serve it with whipped cream, as she does, or with English Cream, a more richly-flavored accompaniment.

2 tablespoons gelatin
2 cups water
⅓ cup orange juice
¼ cup lemon juice
Few grains salt
1 cup sugar
1 cup dark Spanish sherry
¼ cup French brandy

Soften gelatin in ¼ cup cold water. Then add to 1 cup boiling water. Stir until dissolved and smooth. Pour in rest of water, orange and lemon juice, salt, and sugar. Stir to dissolve sugar, then strain. Add sherry and brandy. Pour into a lightly-buttered fluted mold or individual molds. Turn out and serve with:

English Cream

2 cups heavy cream
4 egg yolks
Few grains salt
¼ cup sugar
2-inch piece vanilla bean or 2 teaspoons vanilla extract

Mix 1 cup cream with the egg yolks and beat well. Add salt, sugar, and vanilla bean if using. Pour into top of a double boiler and stir until mixture just coats the spoon—use a wooden spoon if possible. Let cool. Fold in other cup of cream, whipped, and add vanilla extract now if using it. Chill until ready to serve if you wish.

Rice Imperial (6 to 8 servings)

This dessert, said to have been a favorite of Empress Eugenie, is named in her honor. Serve with a fruit topping, with or without spirits. Some appropriate sauces will be found in the Cornucopia of Fruit chapter. I recommend especially the 1830 Orange Compote, Cardinal Peaches or Pears, or the Midsummer Fruit Compote.

½ cup rice
3 cups milk
Few grains salt
1½-inch piece vanilla bean or 2 teaspoons extract
3 egg yolks
½ teaspoon nutmeg
½ to ⅔ cup sugar
1 tablespoon gelatin
1 cup heavy cream
⅓ cup currants (optional)

Put rice in top of a double boiler with 2¾ cups milk, salt, and vanilla bean. (Add extract later.) Cover and cook about 1 hour or until rice is very fluffy and tender. Stir occasionally. When cooked, put rice in a blender or mixer and whip smooth if you like, or use it as is. If using a blender, remove vanilla bean, add in egg yolks. Otherwise, add beaten yolks, nutmeg, sugar, and vanilla extract if using. Soften gelatin in remaining ¼ cup cold milk. Set container over hot water until gelatin melts. Add to rice mixture at once. Fold in whipped cream and currants if you are using them. Taste for flavor, add more sugar if needed. Pour into a lightly-buttered fluted mold, small loaf pan, or a melon mold. Cool and refrigerate until firm. Make this dessert the day before it is to be used. Then turn out on a serving platter and surround with a fruit sauce.

Crème Brûlée or Burnt Cream (6 servings)

Dessert creams, of which this is the finest, were very popular in days gone by. They are still impressive, especially if served in small china pots de crème placed on a tiered china stand. But you can use ramekins, small custard cups, or foil tartlet pans, and achieve an equal elegance. Be sure to chill this dessert in the containers in which it is to be served.

4 egg yolks
2 tablespoons sugar
1 pint heavy cream
Few grains salt
1-inch piece vanilla bean or 1 teaspoon extract
1 cup soft medium-brown sugar (about)

Beat yolks until light and lemon-colored, using an electric mixer if possible. Add sugar and beat until mixture resembles cake batter. Put cream in top of double boiler and allow to boil for just 1 minute, while you stir constantly. Pour *very slowly* over the eggs, return mixture to top of double boiler, add salt, and the vanilla bean if using. Cook until it just coats the spoon, like a thin custard. Do not overcook or it will curdle. Remove from heat, add vanilla extract if using, and pour into cups. Cool and refrigerate overnight or at least 8 hours.

Before serving, sprinkle ½- to ¾-inch layer of brown sugar (free from lumps) over each portion. Glaze under broiler and watch carefully that it does not literally burn. Serve at once or return to the refrigerator until ready. It is delicious by itself, but in the old days it was often accompanied by stewed fruit.

Jellied Zabaglione (6 to 8 servings)

6 egg yolks
1 cup sugar
¾ cup sherry or Marsala
2 tablespoons rum
2 tablespoons lemon juice
Grated rind ½ lemon
1 tablespoon gelatin
4 egg whites
Few grains salt
3 tablespoons sugar

Beat yolks with 1 cup sugar until light and spongy. Reserve 3 tablespoons of wine and add rest to yolks, beating well. Mix in rum, lemon juice, and rind. Pour in double boiler and cook over low heat until mixture just coats the spoon. Stir constantly, using a wooden spoon if possible. Don't overcook or custard will curdle. Remove from stove. While still hot, add in gelatin softened in the 3 tablespoons wine. Stir well until completely dissolved. Cool to room temperature. Fold in egg whites, beaten stiff with salt and mixed with 3 tablespoons sugar. Pour into individual molds or 1 large mold and refrigerate until firm. Serve from the containers or turn out and top with Red Raspberry Purée (see recipe).

Note: If Marsala is used, omit extra 3 tablespoons sugar in egg whites as this wine is sweet.

Italian Cheese Custard (8 servings)

½ pound cream cheese
2 whole eggs
2 egg yolks
Few grains salt
½ cup powdered sugar
½ cup Marsala, Madeira, or sherry
12 ladyfingers or macaroons
Whipped cream
½ cup ground toasted almonds (optional)

Place cheese in a bowl. Using an electric mixer if possible, add in eggs, one at a time, beating until mixture is smooth and free from lumps. Add yolks, salt, and sugar. Taste, adding more sugar if needed. Add in 2 tablespoons of wine.

If using ladyfingers, cut in half. Dip cakes in rest of wine and place around edge of serving dishes or glasses. Pour custard over. Cool and refrigerate until ready to serve. Top each portion with whipped cream, flavored with a little wine, and a tablespoon of ground almonds.

French Mocha-Chocolate Cream (6 servings)

This dessert is one of the masterpieces of the French culinary art. It is simple to make but if you want perfection, use the finest semisweet chocolate you can buy. Never make this with *milk* chocolate.

½ pound semisweet chocolate
1 cup coffee
4 eggs, separated
Few grains salt
2 tablespoons sugar
1 teaspoon vanilla

Melt chocolate with coffee in top of a double boiler. When smooth, remove from the stove, add egg yolks and beat well. Beat whites stiff with salt. Add in sugar and vanilla and beat again. Fold into chocolate mixture and pour at once into pots de crème, ramekins, or custard cups. Chill until firm. You can make this dessert the day before using. Serve plain or top with whipped cream.

Variation: Dorothy Clark makes a heavenly variation, using only ¾ cup coffee and just before pouring mixture into cups, she adds ¼ cup crème de cacao.

SERVE AT WILL

Nassau Syllabub (1 serving)

You will not find a prettier, easier, or more delicious dessert than this one brought back from Nassau by Geraldine Baker. Make it in any container you wish, but she served hers in crystal wine glasses. Put an ounce (2 tablespoons) of guava jelly into each glass. Add an ounce (2 tablespoons) of sherry. Top with a heaping teaspoon of sweetened whipped cream, flavored with vanilla. Or use vanilla ice cream if the dessert does not have to stand.

Caramel Flan (6 ramekins or custard cups)

This is one of the most popular of all Spanish desserts, a rich, velvety baked custard in a jacket of stylish brown caramel. It is really your old friend Crème au Caramel, travelling under another name.

4 eggs
¼ cup sugar
1-inch piece vanilla bean or 1 teaspoon extract
1 cup milk
1 cup light cream or evaporated milk
Few grains salt
½ cup sugar, caramelized

Beat eggs and ¼ cup sugar until light and lemon-colored, using an electric mixer if possible. Add scrapings from split piece of vanilla bean or the extract and other ingredients except caramelized sugar. Beat well. Have ready caramel-lined cups (directions below) and pour mixture in at once. Place in a pan ¼ full of warm water and bake in a 375° F. oven. Cook 30 to 40 minutes or until a knife comes out clean when inserted in center of custard. (Avoid overcooking—it makes a tough, watery custard.) Chill. To serve, loosen edges of custard with a dull knife. Place serving plate over the custard cup and turn upside down, pouring the divine caramel sauce over the custard.

To Line Cups with Caramel: Follow directions for caramelizing sugar in Browning (see recipe in Season to Taste section). When mixture is a clear caramel color, turn off heat. Pour 1 or 2 tablespoons of sirup in each cup, turn it sideways to spread sirup all over inside. This takes practice as you must work quickly or sirup becomes too hard to use. If it does, add ¼ cup water; mixture will lump, but cook until smooth and thick again.

French Strawberry Pudding (6 servings)

1 dozen macaroons
⅔ cup Marsala or sherry
1 pint fresh ripe strawberries
1 cup sugar
4 eggs, separated
1 tablespoon lemon juice
Grated rind of ½ lemon
2 tablespoons sugar

Place a whole macaroon in the bottom of each custard cup or use a quart-sized baking dish, and macaroon halves around the bottom and sides. Pour wine over and saturate cakes. Wash berries, hull, cut in half, and let stand for 10 minutes with ½ cup sugar. Put a layer in cups or baking dish. Beat egg yolks very light with ½ cup sugar. Add lemon juice and rind and beat again, using an electric mixer if handy. In a separate bowl, beat whites very stiff. Fold half of them into the egg yolks and pour over berries. Add 2 tablespoons sugar to remaining egg whites and pile on top. Set cups or baking dish in a pan a quarter full of water and bake in a 350° F. oven for 20 to 25 minutes or until meringue browns. The large pudding may take longer, but the filling should not be too stiff. It is a little on the runny side, but oh, so delectable.

19 A TAZZA OF TASTY TARTS

In the lavish Edward VII era, when formal dinners were an everyday occurrence, miniature tarts and pastries were brought to the table on elaborate silver or crystal tazzas, tall dishes on graceful pedestals. While formality has gone by the board, and the tazza is practically extinct, these dainty tarts have never lost their appeal. An introduction to the modern homemaker is in order: the tarts are easy to prepare, comparatively inexpensive, and, unless their fillings are very runny, they can be picked up and eaten with the fingers, doing away with dessert plates. Best of all, they freeze unusually well, before and after baking.

But there is a secret to making them successfully. They require a very special crust. It must not be so hard or brittle that it shatters at the first bite, nor so soft and flaky that it becomes soggy with standing. I believe the recipe which follows meets those requirements. It is, in my opinion, the dean of all piecrusts. I take great pleasure in presenting to you the venerable:

English Paste (Tart Crust Supreme)

3 nine-inch pies or 4 to 5 dozen tiny tartlets.

3 cups sifted all-purpose flour
1 tablespoon sugar
¾ teaspoon salt
½ teaspoon baking powder
½ cup butter or margarine
½ cup lard or vegetable shortening
1 egg
Milk

Sift dry ingredients. Add fats, softened to room temperature, but not melted. Work with the fingers or pastry blender until mixture resembles coarse bread crumbs. Drop whole egg in a measuring cup and add enough milk to make half a cup. Pour this into fat-and-flour mixture. Knead just long enough to make a stiff paste. If, by any chance, the dough should be too soft (type of flour used might cause a slight difference in consistency), chill in the refrigerator for 30 to 40 minutes, or until it can be easily handled. If too stiff, add a little more milk, a tablespoon at a time. As a rule, the above proportions are perfect. *To cut English Paste recipe in half:* Divide all ingredients by 2, but use 2 tablespoons of the whole egg, beaten, and 2 tablespoons of milk or a little more.

To cut English Paste recipe to a third: Divide all ingredients by 3, but use 1 tablespoon of the whole egg, beaten, and 1 or 2 tablespoons of milk.

Do not substitute the egg yolk for the whole egg; the consistency will not be the same.

To Roll Paste

I divide the paste into three parts and roll out one part at a time. Use a floured board or marble slab and a floured rolling pin. Turn dough once while rolling, using a bit more flour if needed. Roll thin as possible without breaking—about ⅛ inch. Cut out and fit into pans.

Tartlet Pans or an Improvisation

My individual tartlet pans measure 1¾ inches across the bottom, 2¾ inches across the top, and are ⅔ inch deep. These are the sort used by professional bakers and are called Maids of Honor tins in England. Foil pans this size are now on the market.

To improvise, use small muffin pans (the smaller the better). Cut out rounds of dough with a cooky cutter, 2½ to 3 inches should be about right, and if you have a cutter with a scalloped edge, use it. The bottom of the muffin cup must be covered. The dough should extend up the sides about ½ to ⅔ inch—no more. Press dough firmly into the cups with your fingers.

To Chill and Freeze Shells

For best results, this paste must be chilled before baking. I line my pans as soon as dough is rolled out. If shell is to be baked *empty*, prick it all over with a sharp-pronged fork. Be careful not to tear or make large holes. Trim edges, press with a fork or flute.

Put pans either in the refrigerator where paste remains fresh for a week, or in the freezer where, wrapped in foil, it lasts several months. Chill at least 2 hours before baking; overnight is really better.

To Prebake Shells

To be sure the shells remain flat in the center while baking, line them loosely with waxed or heavy brown paper, and fill with dried beans or uncooked rice. Bake 5 minutes in a 450° F. oven, or until done but not browned.

When cooled, remove beans and paper. Fill as directed in the recipes which follow.

To Reheat Frozen Baked Tarts or Shells

Place baked filled tarts or shells, without defrosting, in a fairly hot oven, 400° F., until thoroughly heated. Do not overcook. Let cool to desired temperature.

FILLINGS FOR TARTS

Maids-of-Honor Tarts (18 to 20 tartlets)

It is said that Anne Boleyn, anxious to tempt the jaded appetite of Henry VIII, paid a baker in the little town of Richmond a thousand pounds sterling for this recipe. Delighted, Henry named the tiny pastries *Maids of Honor,* after Anne, who was then Maid of Honor to Queen Catherine.

¼ cup softened butter
½ cup sugar
2 egg yolks
2 tablespoons heavy cream or evaporated milk
Grated rind of ½ lemon
1½ teaspoons lemon juice
¼ teaspoon grated nutmeg
⅔ cup ground, blanched, lightly-toasted almonds
½ cup currants (optional)
¾ teaspoon rose water or use vanilla extract
¾ teaspoon orange flower water or use almond extract

Cream butter and sugar, using an electric mixer if possible. Add egg yolks, one at a time, then the cream or evaporated milk and other ingredients. Blend thoroughly. The mixture will resemble cake batter. Spoon into prebaked tartlet shells (5 minutes in a 450° F. oven or until done but not browned). *Do not fill over ⅔ full;* the filling rises when baking. Bake in a 375° oven from 10 to 20 minutes. Size of tartlet varies baking time. The filling should be cooked, but not hard. Avoid overcooking. Cool before serving.

Note: The original recipe called for rose water and orange flower water. If you can't buy these at the drugstore, use the extracts.

Bakewell Tarts (About 15 tiny tartlets)

These delectable tartlets are named for the English town of Bakewell where they were first sold. They are a variation of Maids of Honor, the only difference being that a well-drained preserved strawberry or ½ teaspoon raspberry or currant jelly is put in the bottom of the prebaked tartlet shell before filling is added. Then currants are omitted.

If larger tarts are used, cover bottom ¼ inch deep with jelly. Baking directions are the same.

Cheese Tarts Royal, 1510 (20 tiny tartlets)

In honor of the coronation of Queen Elizabeth II, Elizabeth Craig, distinguished English author and radio food commentator, published a cookbook called *Court Favorites.* The book was based on a compilation of British royalty's favorite recipes, written out by Queen Victoria. Here is another one Anne Boleyn was partial to—a *cheese* tart without cheese:

To make the curds: Beat 1 whole egg with an egg yolk, using an electric mixer if possible. Add 1 cup of milk and boil in a saucepan, stirring constantly. When mixture curdles and looks like scrambled eggs, pour into a cheese cloth bag or a linen napkin dipped in cold water and wrung dry. Tie securely around top, hang over bowl, let curds drain.

While curds are draining, make English Paste, roll thin, fit it into your pans, chill, and bake 5 minutes in a 450° F. oven. Do not brown. Or prebake refrigerated or frozen shells. When shells cool, curds should be ready—moist, not dry.

⅓ cup butter, softened
¾ cup sugar
⅓ cup cream or evaporated milk
1 tablespoon sherry
1 teaspoon orange flower water
½ teaspoon rose water
½ teaspoon powdered cinnamon
¼ teaspoon grated nutmeg
¼ teaspoon ground coriander seeds
1 tablespoon flour
⅓ cup currants
½ to ¾ cup curds

Cream butter and sugar together. Beat in cream or evaporated milk, sherry, flavorings, spices, and flour, one ingredient at a time. Use an electric mixer if possible. Fold in currants and curds by hand. Fill cooled tartlet shells ⅔ full. Bake in a 350° F. oven until filling *just* sets and no longer shakes. Avoid overcooking. Allow 10 to 12 minutes for the tiny tartlets and 15 to 20 minutes for the larger tarts. Cool before removing from pans. These can be made the morning of the party.

Note: If you cannot buy orange flower water and rose water at the drugstore, substitute vanilla and almond extracts.

Heirloom Chess Tarts (18 to 24 tartlets)

This heirloom recipe came from Rose W. James of New Albany, Indiana. It makes one of the most delicious tartlets. Avoid overcooking. The filling should be a semitransparent, soft jelly which literally melts in your mouth.

1 cup butter or margarine
3 cups sugar
6 egg yolks
2 egg whites
1 teaspoon vanilla
Nutmeg

Soften butter or margarine, cream with sugar, using an electric mixer if possible. Slowly add yolks beaten with whites and continue beating. When ready, mixture resembles cake batter. Place in top of double boiler, have heat high at first, then lower as soon as water in lower part boils. Keep stirring until thick as boiled custard. Remove from heat; add vanilla. Spoon into tartlet shells previously baked 5 minutes at 450° F. Fill ⅔ full and grate a little nutmeg over each. Place in a slow oven, 325°, and bake until filling puffs up and no longer shakes. It is better to cook too little than overcook. Serve as it is or top with a Meringue (see recipe in Irish Lemon Curd Tarts, substituting 1 teaspoon vanilla for the lemon juice and omitting nuts).

My Apple Tarts (About 24 tartlets)

2 cups pared, coarsely-shredded winter apples, packed firm
½ cup water
¾ cup sugar
½ lemon, juice and rind
Few grains salt
2 tablespoons butter, melted
2 tablespoons flour
¼ teaspoon cinnamon
¼ teaspoon nutmeg
2 tablespoons apricot preserves or apricot or peach marmalade

Shred, do not grate the apples. Boil water, sugar, lemon juice, and rind which has been ground with white pulp, for 5 minutes. Mix other ingredients with apples, then combine with sirup. Boil, stirring constantly, until thickened and flour no longer tastes—about 5 minutes. Pour filling in *unbaked* shells to ⅔ full only. Place in a hot oven, 450° F., for 10 minutes. Then lower heat to 350° and bake until crust is browned, filling is bubbly, and apples look transparent—5 to 10 minutes longer. Let cool in pans. Serve plain or with a piece of aged Cheddar cheese.

Orange Curd Tarts (18 to 20 tiny tartlets)

¾ cup butter
1 cup sugar
3 egg yolks
1 cup orange juice
1½ teaspoons grated orange rind
½ teaspoon grated lemon rind
2 tablespoons cornstarch

Cream softened butter and sugar, using an electric mixer if possible. Beat in 1 yolk at a time. Add juice and grated rinds (yellow part only) mixed with cornstarch, and stir. Place in double boiler, have heat high at first, then lower when water boils in bottom part. Never stop stirring. When mixture is consistency of thick custard, set aside to cool. Spoon into tartlet shells previously baked 5 minutes in a 450° F. oven, and top with Meringue (see recipe above but substitute 1 tablespoon orange juice for 1 tablespoon lemon juice and omit nuts.) Bake in a 325° oven until meringue browns, about 10 minutes.

Irish Lemon Curd Tarts (20 to 24 tiny tartlets)

2 whole eggs
2 egg yolks
1½ cups sugar
Grated peel of 4 lemons
⅔ cup lemon juice
1 cup melted butter

Beat whole eggs, yolks, and sugar, using an electric mixer if possible. Add grated peel (yellow part only), juice, and butter, beating all the while. Pour mixture in top of a double boiler. Have heat high, then lower when water in bottom part boils. Keep stirring until mixture is a thick custard. Cool thoroughly before spooning into tartlet shells (previously baked 5 minutes in a 450° F. oven). Top with:

Meringue

4 egg whites
Few grains salt
⅓ cup sugar
2 tablespoons lemon juice
¼ cup ground, toasted, unblanched almonds

Beat whites with salt until stiff enough to stand in peaks. Add sugar slowly and continue to beat, using an electric mixer if possible. Add lemon juice. Spoon over top of tarts and roughen surface. Sprinkle each tart with nuts. Bake in a 325° F. oven until meringue becomes light brown, about 10 minutes. Cool and serve.

Mincemeat Tarts (18 to 20 tartlets)

These have been popular in both England and America for over two hundred years. Use unbaked, chilled, tartlet shells. Fill ⅔ full of well-spiced mincemeat, laced with brandy or rum. Place in a hot oven, 400° F., and bake until filling bubbles and crust is browned, about 15 to 20 minutes.

Fudgies (About 32 tiny tartlets)

These are among the most delicious of all the pick-up or finger pies. They keep for several days in a tin box with a tight-fitting lid. (Freezing is not recommended; no chocolate product seems able to retain its fine flavor.)

½ cup butter
1 cup sugar
2 eggs
2 ounces (2 squares) bitter chocolate
½ cup flour
¼ pound (1 cup) chopped, lightly-toasted pecans or English walnuts
½ teaspoon vanilla

Cream softened butter and sugar, using an electric mixer if handy. Add eggs and beat again. Pour in chocolate, melted in top of double boiler, and mix in flour well. Fold in nuts; add vanilla. Fill tartlet shells, previously baked 5 minutes in a 450° F. oven, ⅔ full. Smooth with back of spoon. Bake 10 minutes in a moderate oven, 350°. Avoid overcooking. Filling will fall a little but no matter. Cool and remove tarts from pans. Decorate with a frosting tube with chocolate icing or:

Jiffy Fudge Frosting

Melt 2 ounces (2 squares) bitter chocolate in double boiler with 2 tablespoons butter. Add 2 tablespoons cream or evaporated milk. Stir in ½ pound (1½ cups) powdered sugar and ½ teaspoon vanilla. Beat to a very stiff paste, but one that can be handled. If too thin, add more sugar; if too stiff, more cream. Spread over cooled Fudgies, or pipe rosettes or flutings onto pastries with a frosting or decorating tube.

20 HOME TOUCHES FOR BOUGHT CAKES

It's the clothes that make the man—it's the fillings and frostings that make the cake. With this in mind, I've compiled a sheaf of recipes for turning spongecake, angel food, orange chiffon, jelly roll, and coffeecake into party desserts. These cakes can be purchased from the grocery or neighborhood bakery, at a negligible cost, and glamourized with home touches. They are then ready to be presented to your most distinguished guests.

MIRACLES WITH SPONGECAKE

Points to remember when purchasing:

1. For the fillings and frostings which follow, buy a single 9-inch layer, 2 to 3 inches high.
2. Select a plain, unfrosted cake without a filling.
3. Be sure no strong flavoring has been added to the batter. In particular, avoid synthetic flavors such as lemon extract and vanillin. It is impossible to camouflage them.

Preparation of Cake for Fillings

Some cakes are baked and sold in paper containers; be careful to remove any paper from the cake. With a saw-toothed bread knife or other knife, cut the layer in half, crosswise, making two even layers. Place the top layer on waxed paper, top side down, for easy transfer to filled bottom layer. Put the bottom layer on the plate the cake will be served on, or cut a cardboard one or two inches larger than the cake, cover it with foil, and place the layer on it. These are fragile cakes and once filled and frosted they cannot be transferred to other dishes without disaster.

Spread the filling evenly and put top layer over it carefully, placing cut side over filling. Handle gently to keep from crumbling. Frost as directed in various recipes below.

Boston Cream Cake (8 servings)

For a plain vanilla filling, use 1 cup of commercially prepared vanilla pudding, fortified (when cooled) with ½ teaspoon vanilla or almond extract.

For a sherry or Madeira-flavored filling, use 1 cup vanilla pudding prepared with a little less milk than called for. Add 2 or 3 tablespoons of wine when cooked pudding is removed from stove. Or make your own custard:

Boston Cream

2 eggs, well beaten
⅓ cup sugar
2 tablespoons flour
1 cup milk or use part cream
2 tablespoons melted butter
1 teaspoon vanilla

To well-beaten eggs, add sugar and flour mixed with milk. Stir in butter and cook in a double boiler until very thick, stirring constantly. When cool, add vanilla. Spread on bottom spongecake layer.

To frost, use Jiffy Fudge Frosting (see recipe). Spread over top and sides of cake. This can be done several hours before serving. If weather is warm, refrigerate until serving time.

Spanish Almond Cake (8 servings)

Flavor 1 cup of vanilla pudding or Boston Cream with ½ teaspoon almond extract, and spread over bottom layer of spongecake. Sprinkle freely with about ⅓ cup unblanched, toasted, grated or ground almonds. Put on top layer and frost:

Almond-Cocoa Frosting

1½ cups powdered sugar
¼ cup cocoa
2 tablespoons melted butter or margarine
½ teaspoon almond extract
¼ teaspoon vanilla
2 or 3 tablespoons cream
½ cup blanched, toasted, coarsely-chopped almonds

Sift sugar and cocoa into a bowl. Add butter or margarine, extracts, and just enough cream to make a frosting soft enough to spread without running. If too soft, add more sugar; if too stiff, more cream. Sprinkle almonds over cake while frosting is still soft.

French Mocha-Praline Cake (8 servings)

⅓ cup sugar
¼ cup flour
1¼ cups milk
1 teaspoon vanilla
½ cup butter or part margarine, softened
1 ounce (1 square) bitter chocolate
½ teaspoon instant coffee
¼ pound French Praline, ground

Sift sugar and flour together. Stir in milk gradually, or mix all in a blender. Pour into a double boiler and cook until thick, stirring constantly. This will look like wallpaper paste when *properly* cooked. Cool to room temperature. Add vanilla. To smooth out any lumps, beat in an electric mixer if handy. Then slowly combine this paste with well-creamed butter. Divide mixture in half, putting into separate bowls. To one bowl, add the melted chocolate, stirring well; to the other, the instant coffee. Spread chocolate mixture, which is the filling, over bottom layer. Put on top layer and frost with the coffee mixture. Sprinkle the candy over the top and sides. Buy candy or make as shown on next page.

French Praline (Almond or Hazelnut Glacé)

Caramelize ½ cup of sugar (see recipe page 19, but omit water and salt). When sugar is a rich brown, free from lumps, quickly stir in ½ cup of unblanched, toasted almonds or hazelnuts. Pour at once onto a lightly-buttered marble slab or china platter. Let cool and harden. Then break up with a kitchen mallet or hammer, and grind through finest blade of the meat grinder. Or wrap praline in a kitchen towel and pound fine with a mallet.

Italian Rum-and-Marron Cake (8 servings)

Brush bottom half of split spongecake with rum—it will take about 2 tablespoons. Spread with about ⅓ cup of marrons, drained of their sirup, and coarsely chopped. (These can be bought at delicatessens or specialty food shops.) Spread the following on top of the marrons:

Rum Cream Filling

⅓ cup sugar
¼ cup flour
1 cup milk
¼ cup rum
1 to 2 tablespoons brandy
½ cup softened butter or part margarine

Mix sugar and flour. Stir in milk gradually, making a smooth paste. Add rum and pour into top of a double boiler. Cook, stirring constantly, preferably with a wooden spoon, until mixture thickens. It should be quite stiff. Set aside, cover, and let cool to room temperature. Add brandy. Pour custard over butter. Then beat hard, with an electric mixer if possible, until light. Taste, adding more rum if needed, and spread over marrons. Put on top layer. Brush it with more rum. Frost with either of the following:

Whipped-Cream-and-Rum Topping

1 cup heavy cream
Few grains salt
1 tablespoon rum or more to taste
2 tablespoons powdered sugar or more

Beat cream with salt; when stiff, fold in rum and powdered sugar to taste. Spread over top and sides of cake and refrigerate until ready to serve.

Uncooked Rum Frosting

1½ cups powdered sugar
2 tablespoons melted butter or margarine
½ teaspoon vanilla
2 tablespoons rum or more
Few grains salt

Sift sugar into mixing bowl. Combine with butter or margarine and vanilla. Add enough rum to make frosting soft enough to spread. Mix salt in. Frost top and sides of cake.

Robert E. Lee Cake, a Lemon Jelly Cake (8 servings)

This is said to have been the General's favorite cake. To make it, put the split spongecake layers together with 1 cup of the filling used for Irish Lemon Curd Tarts (see recipe). Frost with:

Lemon Fluff Frosting

1 egg white
Few grains salt
1½ cups sifted powdered sugar
1 tablespoon lemon juice
½ teaspoon grated lemon rind
⅛ teaspoon cream of tartar

Beat egg white stiff with salt. Gradually add sugar, beating constantly, with an electric mixer if possible. Add lemon juice and rind mixed with cream of tartar. Continue to whip until stiff. Spread over top and sides of cake. Roughen surface and set aside to harden.

Zuppa Inglesa, an Italian Rum-Fruit Cake (8 servings)

In Italy, this is a very popular dessert. Make it exactly like the Italian Rum-and-Marron Cake but substitute mixed crystallized or dried fruits for the marrons. Use candied orange and lemon peels, angelica, citron, currants, raisins, cherries, pineapple, etc., soaked overnight in rum or brandy. One third cup of mixed fruits should absorb 2 or 3 tablespoons of liquor.

ANGEL GLAMOUR CAKES

The home touches for the luscious cakes which follow are based on a 12-egg (1-pound) angel-food cake.

Strawberry Dream Cake (12 servings)

This is one of Isabel McMeekin's specialties. With a sharp knife, cut an inch-thick slice from the top of the angel cake. Next, make an inch-wide shell of the cake by removing most of the center part with kitchen scissors or forks. Place cake shell on serving platter or foil-covered cardboard. Plug up center hole with a piece of cake, pressing edges to seal. Fill the shell with cake pieces and cover with:

Strawberry Cream

1 tablespoon gelatin
2 tablespoons cold water
1 pint frozen strawberries, defrosted, or fresh ones mixed with ½ cup sugar
1 tablespoon lemon juice
1 cup heavy cream
Few grains salt

Soften gelatin in the cold water. Place container over hot water and cook until gelatin melts. Meanwhile purée berries or whip in a blender. Add gelatin and lemon juice. Fold in cream whipped with salt; taste for sweetness adding more sugar if needed. Refrigerate until mixture begins to jell. Do not let get too stiff. Whip with a fork and pile on top of angel-cake pieces in the shell. Set the top slice over this; secure it with picks. Refrigerate until a few hours before serving. Frost with:

Whipped Cream Frosting

2 cups heavy cream
1 teaspoon vanilla
⅓ cup powdered sugar or more
Berries for garnish if in season

Whip cream well, adding in vanilla and powdered sugar. Frost cake and garnish with berries.

Note: Red raspberries may be substituted for strawberries.

Pink Perfection Peppermint Cake (12 servings)

This is one of the prettiest and most delicious of the glamourized angel cakes. Cut off a top slice and make a shell as for Strawberry Dream Cake (see recipe above). Use just enough cake bits to fill up the hole in the bottom of the shell. Fill with:

Pink Peppermint Cream

½ pound peppermint stick candy
1 cup light cream
Few grains salt
1 tablespoon gelatin
2 tablespoons cold water
1 cup heavy cream

Crush the candy and put in top of double boiler with the light cream and salt. Set over high heat and when water boils, lower heat. Cover and cook until candy melts, stirring occasionally—20 to 30 minutes. Mix gelatin with cold water.

Let soften a minute, then add to hot peppermint mixture. Stir until smooth; if lumps appear, strain. Cool to room temperature. Whip the heavy cream stiff, but not buttery. Fold into cooled peppermint mixture and spoon into the cake shell. If filling does not reach the top, add cake pieces until it is level. Put top slice on, secure with picks, and refrigerate cake overnight or longer. An hour or so before serving frost with one of the following:

Circus-striped Whipped Cream Frosting

2 cups heavy cream
⅓ cup powdered sugar or more to taste
¼ pound peppermint stick candy, crushed
2 ounces chocolate sprinkles or shaved semisweet chocolate

Whip the cream stiff enough to stand in peaks but do not overbeat. Add sugar. Spread over top and sides of cake. Make alternate stripes of peppermint and chocolate candy over the top of the cake with a rim of peppermint candy around the edge. Chill until serving time.

Cocoa Cream Frosting

2 cups heavy cream
¾ cup powdered sugar or more to taste
Few grains salt
½ cup cocoa
1 teaspoon vanilla
2 ounces chocolate sprinkles or shavings semisweet chocolate (optional)

Whip cream stiff but not buttery. Add sugar and salt. Fold in the cocoa and add vanilla. Taste, adding more sugar if necessary. Spread over top and sides of cake. Decorate with chocolate sprinkles or shavings if desired. Refrigerate until serving time.

FAVORITE DESSERT CAKES

Orange Chiffon Cake with Orange Cordial Frosting
(12 servings)

For this elegant frosting, buy a 1-pound orange chiffon cake. Place it on a serving dish or foil-covered cardboard. Pile the frosting on thickly.

Orange Cordial Frosting

1 pound powdered sugar
¼ cup melted butter or margarine
1 teaspoon grated orange peel
2 tablespoons concentrated frozen orange juice
2 tablespoons curaçao
3 or 4 tablespoons Triple Sec, Grand Marnier, or Cointreau

Sift sugar into a mixing bowl. Add butter or margarine, peel, orange juice, and curaçao. Stir well. Add enough of one of the other orange cordials to make a frosting soft enough to spread—not too runny or too stiff. Spread over top and sides of cake. When frosting is sufficiently hardened, refrigerate the cake or store in a tin box with a tight lid. This cake remains fresh up to two weeks. The frosting never gets grainy but stays soft and creamy.

Ice Cream Roll (6 servings)

Hortense Dreyfus introduced me to this really professional-looking dessert. Make it at least 24 hours before serving. It must be stored in the freezer.

1 pound jelly roll or a flat rectangle of spongecake
1 pint vanilla ice cream

If you can buy the spongecake before it is rolled, so much the better. If not, buy the jelly roll. On a sheet of waxed paper, gently unroll, jelly side up. Try not to break the cake, but if you do, the matter isn't serious. Scrape out jelly with a dull knife and spread ice cream over the cake as evenly as possible. Don't let the ice cream melt; work quickly. Using the end of the paper to help, roll cake over ice cream, making it firm. Wrap in waxed paper and put on a flat surface in the freezer. When firm, wrap in foil over the waxed paper, and fold edges to seal. Store until ready to use.

To serve, slice on a bread board using a bread knife. Divide into 6 portions. Top with any sauce you wish. I'm partial to:

Hot Fudge Sauce:

2 ounces (2 squares) bitter chocolate
½ cup milk or water
1 tablespoon butter or margarine
1 cup sugar
Few grains salt
1 teaspoon vanilla

Put chocolate and milk or water in top of double boiler. Cover and cook until chocolate melts. Stir to a smooth paste; add butter or margarine. Mix well, and add sugar and salt. Cook 15 to 20 minutes or until thick. Just before serving, add vanilla. Serve in a sauceboat or pour over each portion.

Variation: Instead of vanilla, you can add rum, Cointreau, or crème de menthe to the Hot Fudge Sauce. Add to taste, starting with 2 tablespoons.

Easy Rum Baba (6 servings)

Buy an 8-inch spongecake or coffeecake made of cupcake or plain cake batter. It does not matter if the cake is topped with cinnamon streusel or a cinnamon-and-nut mixture. Place cake on a serving platter with fairly high sides, as sauce will collect in the bottom. Pour Rum Sauce over the cake at least half an hour before serving—longer would not hurt.

Rum Sauce:

1/3 cup sugar
1/3 cup water
2/3 cup white rum or mild Bacardi rum

Mix sugar and water and boil 3 minutes. Cool. Add rum and pour over cake. Keep spooning over until all liquor is absorbed.

INDEX